PIRATES OF NEW ENGLAND

PIRATES OF NEW ENGLAND

Ruthless Raiders and Rotten Renegades

GAIL SELINGER

Guilford, Connecticut

Globe
Pequot

An imprint of Rowman & Littlefield

Distributed by NATIONAL BOOK NETWORK

British Library Cataloguing in Publication Information available

Library of Congress Cataloging-in-Publication Data
Names: Selinger, Gail, author.
Title: Pirates of New England : ruthless raiders and rotten renegades / Gail
   Selinger.
Description: Guilford, Connecticut : Globe Pequot, an imprint of Rowman &
   Littlefield, 2017. | Includes bibliographical references and index. |
   Identifiers: LCCN 2017021676 (print) | LCCN 2017021776 (ebook) | ISBN
   9781493029303 (ebook) | ISBN 9781493029297 (pbk.)
Subjects: LCSH: Pirates—New England—History—18th century.
Classification: LCC F7 (ebook) | LCC F7 .S454 2017 (print) | DDC 974/.02—dc23 LC record
   available at https://lccn.loc.gov/2017021676

∞™ The paper used in this publication meets the minimum requirements of American National Standard for Information Sciences—Permanence of Paper for Printed Library Materials, ANSI/ NISO Z39.48-1992.

Printed in the United States of America

To Shelly Shipper

You know why.

Contents

Acknowledgments

IN WRITING THIS NONFICTION BOOK I ENDEAVORED NOT TO RECORD simply a series of dry facts concerning the lives of these pirates. Hopefully I have succeeded. There are a number of people I wish to thank for their support. I raise a full tankard of rum to them.

My husband, Captain Erik H. Berliner, who checked my nautical information for accuracy. His patience, understanding, and love are always there even through my toughest days.

Denise Little for daring to suggest all those years ago that my personal knowledge of pirate history could lead to something.

Susan Williams, friend and computer guru, who got me through a forty-eight-hour computer near-death experience. Thankfully we all survived.

Sara Ameri, Claudette Guy, Lin Kings, Denise Little, Joan Salisbury, Shelly Shipper, and Pat Summers. You were all there when I needed you the most.

Cindy Vallar, author and pirate historian, and Maria Blumberg of the Huntington Library and Gardens for their expertise when I needed help verifying historical facts.

My sister Carol Sue. She has always been my cheerleader, editor, and best friend. In my childhood she was the person who got me hooked on the lives and histories of these interesting pirate women and men.

Any erroneous historical information sits solely on my shoulders.

Fair winds and smooth sailing. I am Gail Selinger at piratesandmore@yahoo.com.

Author's Note on Wages, Cost of Living, and Pirate Booty

WHEN DISCUSSING PIRATE HISTORY ONE OF THE FIRST QUESTIONS people inevitably ask is, "How much is pirate treasure worth today?"

The biggest obstacle in translating the value of pirate booty from the seventeenth and eighteenth centuries is multilayered. To make a precise monetary equivalent of a pirate's "take" in twenty-first-century money is not truly possible. However, a rough estimation can be achieved.

During the time these pirates lived, the US dollar did not exist. When US currency was officially minted in 1783, the British one-pound sterling note had the purchasing power of five US dollars. I have used this ratio when estimating monetary values.

For the reader to get a better perspective of the disproportionate amounts being transported on seized vessels to wages or goods of the general public, I have used the historic standard of living.

Though there might be a few similarities, the exact goods available in the seventeenth and eighteenth centuries cannot be purchased today. Quantities of items were extremely limited. Everything had to be produced by hand. For example, women hand-stitched clothes, as the first sewing machine was not invented until 1790.

With wages so low in that time, a great many items could be purchased with one penny. Lodging and food were relatively cheaper than today. Other items such as imported cloth, fine clothes—such as a wealthy man's brocade coat—or a pair of shoes came with very high price tags.

Before decimalization in 1970, the denomination of currency in Britain broke down to:

4 farthings = 1 penny (called a pence, written as *d.*).

2 half pennies, called ha'pennies = 1 penny (pence).

12 pennies (pence) = 1 shilling (written as *s.*).

20 shillings = 1 pound (written as £).

£1 = 20s = 240d, means 1 pound is equivalent to 20 shillings or 240 pence (pennies).

10 shillings and 6 pence = 1/2 guinea.

21 shillings = 1 guinea.

For example, if I purchased a man's wig for the amount of one pound, fifteen shillings, and one penny, the price tag would read £1.15.1 or £1.15s.1d.

The Spanish piece of eight, an eight-reale silver coin, was in heavy circulation in the North American colonies. It had the same purchasing power as one English pound.

To entice men onto a blue-water voyage (a long ocean journey), a minimum of one month's wage was paid in advance. Because it was widely known that the life and work on a merchantman ship was harsh, the advance lured men to sign on. This tactic did not always work to a ship owner's advantage. It was not an uncommon occurrence for men to desert at the first port once they had received their pay. The more common payment arrangement was percentages of their wage doled out at various points in a ship's journey, with the final payment made upon return to the home port.

The political climate, as it does even to this day, influenced wages and prices. Prices went up during wartime. Commodities were harder to get. The economic and political influence of individuals with wealth was great. Since there was less of everything in those centuries, according to historian Jan Rogoziński "a man with £500 cash in his pocket possessed more wealth than 99 percent of the population of Europe and North America."

Below I have listed the wages of a ship's crew throughout the eighteenth century. All values are for monthly wages unless otherwise stated.

Captains of varied ship sizes received £5 to £6.

Captains of large vessels, such as those run by the East India Company, received £10.

First mate or mate received £3.63 to £4.38.

Second mate (only on a large ship) received £2.50 to £3.

Carpenter received £3.08 during peace and £4.09 during war. If teaching an apprentice, he would receive an additional £2 or £3.

Surgeon received £3.06 during peace and £4.09 during war.

Boatswain (the petty officer) received £2.52 during peace and £3.20 during war.

Gunner received £2.10 during peace and £3.20 during war.

Cooper (the builder of wooden barrels) received £2.07 during peace and £2.80 during war.

Sailmaker, caulker, and armorer received £2 to £3 a month.

Cook received £1.62 during peace and £2.40 during war.

Able-bodied seaman (a.k.a. able seaman), a man with over two years' experience sailing as a deck hand, received £1.65 during peace and £2.58 during war.

Foremastman (a.k.a. common tar, a.k.a. common seaman) received £1.46 during peace and £2.20 during war.

Merchant seaman received £1.32 to £2.60.

Ship's boy (a.k.a. cabin boy, a.k.a. servant to ship's officers) received 4s.17d.

Army and navy recruitment sign-on bonus was 1s.

As a wage comparison, a household servant directly below that of butler received £4 to £5 yearly. An unskilled laborer received 9s. per week.

I have listed below the cost of a variety of foods and goods able to be purchased in the port of London in 1700.

1 quart single ale or beer sealed . . . . .4d.

1 quart best ale or beer sealed . . . . .6d.

½ loaf of bread. . . . . .1d.

1 pound cheese domestic . . . . 4d.–6d.

Enough gin to get intoxicated . . . . .1d.

Enough gin to get dead drunk. . . . . .2d.

1 quart best claret. . . . . .6d.

1 pound butter . . . . 8d.–10d.

1 pound fatty bacon . . . . .10d.–1s.

1 pound candles . . . . .2s.6d.

1 pound coffee . . . . 4s.9d.–6s.

1 capon (chicken). . . . . 1s.

1 pound tea . . . . 7s.6d.–16s.

1 dozen rabbits at market . . . . 7s.

1 pound lye soap . . . . 1½d.

1 quart best quality bottle of port . . . . .6d.

1 sealed bottle of white wine . . . . .1s.–8d.

1 tavern meal of bread, cheeses, beer (quantity unknown) . . .2d.

1 bed, 1 man, 1 night . . . . .1d.

1 yard rich brocade satin . . . . .18s.6d.

1 piece (14½ yards) of Indian Spring Muslin . . . . 9s.

1 pair men's yarn stockings . . . . .3s.2d.

1 pair men's silk stockings . . . . .17s.4d.

1 pair "stout" shoes . . . . 7s.

1 pair men's lace ruffles . . . . 16s.

It is no wonder men took their chances at going "on the account," given that wages and goods at home were so meager and their own life choices so limited.

Introduction: The Evolution of Piracy

MOST PEOPLE TODAY BELIEVE PIRATES FIRST CAME INTO BEING toward the end of the seventeenth century, considered by historians to be the beginning of the Golden Age of Piracy. It was a time when the European countries of England, France, Spain, Portugal, and the Netherlands were vying for the riches of the New World. However, from the moment man learned how to tie logs together and sail the waters there have been pirates.

The earliest mention of pirates is inscribed on a clay cuneiform tablet found in the town of Ugarit, on the coast of Syria. These pirates were a combination of tribes dubbed by locals as the Northern Sea People. Between 1220 BCE and 1186 BCE, they consistently attacked the shipping commerce of Egypt, Syria, Crete, Phoenicia, and Cyprus, using the rocky terrain and watery inlets as prime areas for sneak attacks. They terrorized villages along the coast, stealing whatever they wished and capturing townspeople to sell at various slave markets along the way.

It took a massive sea battle in 1186 BCE, spearheaded by Egyptian Pharaoh Ramses III and his naval fleet, to finally end their terror. A carved bas-relief commemorating this victory is considered to be the first pictorial representation of a sea battle. It can be viewed on a temple wall near the modern-day city of Luxor.

With the establishment in the eighth century of the various independent Greek city-states vying for power and control over land and trade routes, piracy once again reemerged, stronger than ever. By the third or fourth century BCE, the Greeks coined a specific name for these marauders: *peirates*, meaning "one who attacks." So fierce were these men, city-states paid pirates not only to collect tribute from a weaker city, but to provide protection if they themselves were attacked. With this practice becoming commonplace, pirates became more brazen by kidnapping high-ranking citizens for ransom.

By this time pirates were so numerous, and their attacks so frequent, that commerce along the Mediterranean nearly stopped. Greek city-states were forced to align in a combined attempt to rid the waters of their constant threat. This only fueled the pirates' wrath, and as a result they created one of the most brutal, torturous deaths for a captive: keelhauling, a crime that is erroneously attributed as being invented by pirates of the seventeenth century.

To keelhaul a captive, pirates would tie his hands and feet with two long lengths of rope and throw the victim overboard. They would then pull the ropes across the ship's deck from bow to stern a number of times, dragging their captive underwater the entire length of the ship, scraping his body along the ship's wooden hull while drowning him at the same time.

Needless to say, the Greek city-states weren't successful in eliminating the pirate threat. It wasn't until 331 BCE that Alexander the Great's naval general Amphoterus was able to stop their murderous activities, only to have piracy slowly reemerge after Alexander's death in 323 BCE.

The constant struggles between the Greek city-states and their inability to permanently defend themselves from pirates helped lead to the collapse of the Greek Empire and the emergence of the Roman Empire as a far greater power in the world. Although the Roman Empire was the strongest military power on land, the Romans neglected to secure their commercial water routes and discovered that they, too, had to contend with pirates attacking in large numbers.

Now calling these men and women *piratia* or *piraicos*, meaning "of or belonging to a pirate or robber on the sea," the Roman Empire was stymied. The government tried everything from constant sea battles to political ploys to end pirate attacks. Diplomats would guarantee to protect lands against the marauding pirates if settlements and cities agreed to join the Roman Empire. This tactic was successfully used in 229 BCE on the settlements along the Adriatic and Ionian Seas against the pirate queen Teuta, who previously had run roughshod over the area.

Even future emperors were not immune from the threat of pirates. In 75 BCE, on his way to Rhodes, Caius Julius Caesar, then a young man in his twenties, was captured at sea by the pirate fleet of Spartaco and held for ransom. Outraged that they asked such a meager price of twenty talents (31 kilograms of gold weight) for his return, Caesar flippantly remarked that he was worth more than a mere twenty, suggesting they demand fifty talents for his release. The pirates quickly agreed to the suggestion. After pillaging the Roman galley, they released the vessel to resume its journey and deliver the ransom request.

The pirate island of Pharmacusa, off the coast of Caria, in Asia Minor, was a large pirate settlement. With his physician, Cinna, and his personal slaves, Caesar remained their hostage for months. Once the ransom was paid and before departing the island, he acknowledged that Spartaco had treated him and his associates kindly. Caesar then informed Spartaco that when he ascended to power he would capture all of them. But he would make sure Spartaco's death was swift and painless. It would take a number of years, but Caesar made good on his word.

It was not until 36 BCE that Emperor Octavian, with a series of combined land and naval attacks, eradicated piracy from the waterways of the Mediterranean, an achievement that would stand for more than three hundred years. But at beginning of what is now called the Dark Ages, piracy reemerged with devastating consequences throughout Europe from an area unknown to most at that time, the Viking North.

Except for a few minor raids, Vikings were virtually unknown in Western Europe. That all changed on June 8, 793 CE, when Vikings who appeared to have risen from hell itself attacked the island of Lindisfarne, situated off the northern coast of England. They looted the monastery situated on the island, which housed one of the richest repositories of church wealth in all of England. After slaughtering monks, taking captives, and stealing all of the wealth stored within, they sailed away before the island's alarm bell could even be rung. The Viking age of terror fell upon Europe for the next three hundred years. In that time Viking pirates would sweep across half of the continent, changing its geographic, economic, and ethnic dynamic forever.

Unable to quell the onslaught of the Vikings, European kings and princes wisely acknowledged their power and presence and made peace offers of land, title, wealth, and even their daughters in marriage.

One such marriage was that of pirate Rollo Ragnvald (a.k.a Rolf Hrolf). In 911CE, Rollo set his sights on the riches of France. He was easily able to conquer the lands along the River Seine. His large force of *Normands* (or "men of the North," as the French called them) sailed up the Seine and besieged Paris to near starvation. King Charles III brokered a treaty with Rollo. He granted Rollo the valley of the lower Seine, the title of duke, and his daughter, Princess Gisla, in marriage, on the promise that Rollo would defend France from any and all future invaders. Thus Rollo became the Duke of Normandy in the province of Normandy (land of the men of the North). The Viking invasion of Europe ended in the late eleventh century. Piracy diminished, though it was never completely eradicated.

Beginning in the thirteenth century, England, France, and Spain engaged each other in a series of naval wars and uneasy treaties, leaving much of their countries' commercial shipping to suffer at the hands of an ever-increasing number of pirates from every Western European country. That century also saw the legal creation of the English privateer under King Henry III. In 1243 Henry III issued the first military letters of marque. The term is derived from the Latin *marcare*, meaning "seize as a pledge," and from the Old French *marque*, meaning "seizure of goods." The letters allowed any man or ship to attack with impunity any and all ships of an enemy nation. Within these legal documents was a pledge that the king would receive half of all the plunder acquired. This helped King Henry to not only lower taxes on his already financially strapped countrymen, but also have the money to rebuild his navy.

With the Viking invasion of France in the ninth century, the ship merchants and sailors of Brittany (a province on the northwest coast of France) took up arms against the Viking raiders. A tradition of noble seafaring fighters was passed down through generations. These families were dubbed *la course* or *corsaire*, derived from the Latin *cursa* or *cursus*, meaning "voyage after plunder," later anglicized to *corsair*. By the thirteenth century, the French corsair, unlike the English privateer, did not require a legal document to assist the navy in the pursuit of his country's enemies. He loyally defended France and her ships when called upon.

⸺◆⸺

We know the story of Columbus and his quest, funded by the king and queen of Spain, to find a shorter water route to India. On October 12, 1492, Christopher Columbus sighted an unknown island, which he named San Salvador. For Western European countries, his discovery of the "New World" changed everything.

Using native guides from the Taino tribe, Columbus explored the islands he was to name San Salvador and Hispaniola (now known as Haiti and the Dominican Republic) and claimed them as the property of Spain. Noticing the gold jewelry adorning the native Arawak Indians of Hispaniola and told the gold stone was easily acquired, Columbus knew he had stumbled across an easy source of wealth for himself and Spain.

Columbus returned with proof of his success and laid the items out before the royal court. Amazed at the abundance of these riches—jewelry, gold nuggets, exotic parrots and fruits, and native slaves—King Ferdinand and Queen Isabella agreed to mount a larger expedition of discovery and conquest.

To guarantee that the Spanish claim be the first legitimate one, King Ferdinand requested a blessed edict from Pope Alexander VI. Declared in 1493, the edict granted Spain the right of complete sovereignty. This covered any and all lands that Columbus had or would discover within a radial longitude of 320 miles west of the Cape Verde Islands, situated off the western coast of Africa.

The Pope was thrilled to grant the edict, as he saw it as a way to Christianize all "heathen people" that Columbus encountered, people who would eventually become subjects of Vatican edicts. It would also bring into the church coffers a percentage of all the wealth found in these new lands through the church's tithe system.

This news did not sit well with the rest of Western Europe. Portugal was especially furious and believed that, as a devoutly Catholic nation, it too should receive a papal edict for a portion of the newly discovered land. On June 7, 1494, under extreme pressure from Portugal, Pope Alexander VI brokered the Treaty of Tordesillas with the two Catholic countries. Spain agreed to move the invisible line of its holdings approximately 933 miles west of the Cape Verde Islands. This enabled Portugal to claim the entire country of Brazil under the papal jurisdiction. Therefore, Portugal was assured that Brazil would never be attacked by Spain.

King Francis I of France believed his country had as much right to any lands and treasure in this new land as the Catholic countries. Even as he sent an official protest to the pope, Francis commissioned his privateering corsairs to set sail immediately to the Caribbean.

By this time King Henry VII of England had achieved peace with France. With a severely depleted wartime navy and treasury, he needed to find a way to rebuild the navy and refill his coffers. While King Francis sent protests to the pope, King Henry quietly issued privateering letters of marque to whoever wished to undertake the voyage. Henry intended to wait and see if indeed the New World held as much wealth as the rumors suggested.

Pirates from every nation, not caring whose ship they attacked, followed the wild stories and sailed to the Caribbean, now referred to as the Spanish Main or the Main, to find out for themselves. To their delight, the wild stories and hushed rumors of untold wealth were true.

Chapter One

Why Turn to Piracy?

WHY WOULD SOMEONE CHOOSE TO RISK HIS LIFE AND TURN PIRATE?
There are many reasons, all of which are anything but straightforward.

Between the fifteenth and eighteenth centuries, wars between
England, France, Portugal, the Netherlands, and Spain were so frequent they became the normal way of life for the average citizen. The
power struggle for religious and commercial world dominance played
out in the theater of the royal courts and religious institutions with
little regard for the everyday citizenry.

Spain by the sixteenth century had established a commercial and
naval stranglehold along the length of the Spanish Main. In 1554,
Queen Mary I of England, Elizabeth's Catholic half-sister (not Mary
of Scotland), and Philip of Spain entered into a political marriage,
hoping to add England to Spain's sphere of influence. Now England
was further divided into the powerful religious factions of the Roman
Catholic Church and the Protestant Church of England. When Mary
died in 1558, her will stated that, legally, since Philip, now King of
Spain, was also her husband, he should ascend the throne of England
as rightful king. Philip viewed this as his royal destiny.

However, the English council, made up of a majority of Protes-
tants, feared if indeed this were to occur, religious persecutions would
escalate. Therefore, the council crowned the Protestant Elizabeth I

queen. Since Elizabeth ascended the throne at a young age, Philip believed he could still achieve his goal by proposing marriage. With her numerous refusals to his "romantic" attempts, Philip's admiration for her turned to hatred. By refusing him, she understood that he would eventually attempt to secure her throne through military force. Elizabeth wasn't incorrect in her assessment, for Spain began to covertly ferment insurrection in the heavily Catholic countries of Scotland and Ireland.

From previous years of military encounters, Elizabeth was faced with a badly depleted national treasury and weakened military. Needing time to build up both the royal treasury and naval forces, she used her political brilliance to diplomatically avoid war with Spain until 1588. On May 19 of that year, King Philip II launched his heavily armed armada across the English Channel to finally conquer England. Through a combination of clever British naval maneuvers and the severe, unpredictable winds of the channel, the armada was destroyed. Any vessel remaining afloat returned to Spain in defeat.

After the war triumphant ships returned to English harbors, where hundreds of sailors intended to disembark. But typhus and fatal dysentery had spread quickly through the English fleet during the weeks of fierce fighting. Officials in the cities realized they had no facilities to help the sick or house the healthy.

City officials provided additional rations to feed the men but forced the weary and sick sailors to remain aboard the fleet ships for weeks. The diseases continued to spread due to overcrowding, filth, and lack of medical care for the contagious men. When finally allowed to disembark, the survivors discovered that no one would offer them rooms. The streets became their only home.

And yet military recruitment continued. With a huge percentage of injuries and deaths occurring during sea voyages, there was a constant demand for men to enter the naval service to meet the conscription quotas.

To understand why piracy reemerged and flourished, it helps to understand everyday life for the common man in places such as England.
Toward the middle of the fifteenth century, considered the Age of
Enlightenment, serfdom began to slowly disappear in countries such
as England. The idea of choosing one's livelihood, and seeking a guaranteed wage, drew many men and boys from the rural countryside's
tenant estates and villages. They hoped to make something of themselves by relocating to cities and port towns. However, opportunities
for employment were not what they expected.

Guilds ran the majority of stores and trade shops. A person
needed to apply first for an apprenticeship at his chosen guildhall.
Working for years and receiving little to no pay, the apprentice hoped
to become a master at the craft, which would enable him to open his
own establishment.

For many born to the lowest social strata, joining the navy to
become a fully trained sailor was the only guarantee of wages and
employment. Others joined for the lure of adventure or to escape the
law. The navy, desperate for sailors, would have thieves and murderers
released from local gaols (jails) and led directly to naval ships to serve
out their sentences. Also, debtors who owed less than £20 sterling
($10,000) in a combined or single debt could escape the fate of prison
if they agreed to join the navy.

Other sources of bodies able to fill a naval compliment were
the many orphanages and desperate parents who sold their boys for
money. Boys as young as 8 years would be signed on as servants or
cabin boys. That age was considered optimum, for they could understand all the regulations and react quickly in urgent situations.

The so-called street urchins running free throughout cities had
two options available for survival: enter the underground criminal
element or go dockside looking for work on a ship. Boys were assets at
sea for their height, speed, and dexterity, and during combat situations

they served a vital role as "powder monkeys." Aboard ship the highly volatile gunpowder was stored loose in wooden barrels. To be as safe as possible, the barrels were stored in their own dry room, called the powder magazine, powder room, or magazine. This room was situated on the lowest deck (the orlop deck). Extreme care was required in and around the room. The loose powder was so volatile, only the powder master assembled the explosive-filled paper cartridges and only prior to a combat encounter. Once a canvas or leather canister was filled with loaded cartridges, a boy rushed it up all the companionways (stairs) to the gun decks, making sure the powder within didn't spill, get damp, or get near any flame. This was by no means a safe or easy job.

This experience on naval and merchant ships would elevate a boy's standing if he ever wished to join pirates. No longer would he be considered a mere servant or cabin boy, but a full crew member and thus entitled to a rightful share in any prizes seized.

In England, at every port city, the naval admiralty established an impress service. The regulations governing this service stated that the appointed regulating officer and his crew could lawfully seize any man between the ages of 18 and 55, no matter what his occupation or status, for service to the Royal Navy.

And so the dreaded press-gangs roamed the port cities with impunity, able to physically force males into service, using whatever means they thought necessary. If a press-ganged individual came from a wealthy family, he had a chance to pay his way out of the conscription by bribing the impress service men.

The admiralty guaranteed to pay a fee to the impress officer for every person he delivered to a ship. Under English law, by accepting a shilling coin ($25), a man legally and instantly volunteered himself into service to the Crown. Whether the man was conscious or not, a shilling would be found in his possession. It took no time at all for the existence of press-gangs to be known throughout the harbors.

Since a man-of-war could be seen on the horizon hours before docking, a city alarm would sound and potential targets would rush to hide as best they could. Though press-gangs were sanctioned to enter any home or business looking for able-bodied men, it soon became harder for them to find anyone. Thus the impress service traveled deeper into the country's farming communities. It became an easier task to grab men unaware of press-gangs. This helps explain why so many Welshmen were registered in the naval musters and named in pirate trials of the time.

If any man, once aboard a naval ship, tried to escape from its hellish conditions, he would be considered a mutineer, tracked down, and executed. The naval courts considered the man guilty whether he had been forced into the navy or truly volunteered for service.

Seamen aboard merchant ships soon discovered they were not exempt from press-gangs. Legally, a naval captain could freely board any ship and conscript as many men as he saw fit. By law, he was required to leave as many men as necessary aboard to enable the vessel to sail on its original voyage. This did not always happen, putting untold physical stress on the men remaining.

For the impress service the easiest places to find "volunteers" became the many taverns and alehouses. The method was simple: Start a drunken brawl with the intended victim, then either beat him unconscious or drag him out in chains.

Another brilliant setup was the tankard/shilling entrapment. Unscrupulous barkeeps, being bribed by an impress representative, would covertly drop a shilling into a tankard before it was served. When the customer realized there was something in his drink and fished out the coin, he would immediately be approached by the press-gang and informed that by touching the coin he had accepted the Crown's pay in advance.

This worked quite well until word spread concerning this ploy. Before they raised their tankard to drink, men began to stir the liquid with any object they had on them. If a coin was discovered, a new drink would be ordered, and the patron would check once more for the evasive shilling until he was satisfied. Once that occurred the men of the press-gang could merely wait until their intended target raised his tankard to drink. With his view obstructed by the solid bottom of the tankard, they would rush their victim.

However, honest tavern keepers began to lose business. To quell the tide, the glass-bottomed tankard was introduced. Not only was a patron able to check whether there was a shilling hidden in his brew, but the glass afforded an unobstructed view, giving the mark a slim chance to elude an attacker.

It did not matter if a man volunteered for service or was press-ganged; the naval captain basically owned him. Along with the long list of naval regulations, a sailor needed to abide by each captain's own set of rules. With complete control over his men and ship, a captain rarely had to account for any actions he took with regard to his men.

A sadistic, psychopathic captain who took great delight in tormenting, torturing, or even killing his sailors ruled without fear of reprisals. With such complete control, no officer under him had any authority to stop such behavior lest he turn his captain's cruelty onto himself. It took a brave sailor to report such cruelties to the High Court of the Admiralty. He had to be willing to surrender a large portion of his wages and acquire legal representation. Though rare, there are historic trial accounts given by titled naval officers against such captains.

Even if a captain was a fair-minded person, life at sea was filled with hard work, little sleep, poor rations, and cramped and filthy insect-ridden, rat-infested quarters. Sailors also had to contend with unexpected storms or attacks. A man would be released from service only when officially informed his enlistment time was up.

Under these conditions, captains feared possible mutiny. All handheld weapons, such as swords, rifles, and flintlock pistols, were stored below deck in a locked cabinet or room. Only a handful of trusted officers carried keys.

Desertion or mutiny became the only options of escape afforded sailors. It proved easier to slip away from a naval ship than attempt to get an entire crew to agree to a full mutiny. To eliminate this temptation many captains forbade their crews from going ashore. Records tell of crews locked below deck with armed officers guarding them while the ship was resupplied and made ready to sail. Thus mutiny was the only choice if disgruntled seamen wanted to take over a merchant ship, declare themselves free of their contracts, and sail away as pirates.

What became of the honest sailor? After a peace treaty was declared, the naval ships sailed home and thousands of men poured back into cities. When attempting to collect their past wages due, nine out of ten were told the country's treasury was drained. They were penniless. For able-bodied men the only options open to them were the merchant lines. So many men applied for those jobs that the captains could drive wages down to starvation level and men would still sign on.

And history repeated itself on land. To the ordinary citizenry, the influx of these leather-tanned men, with their strange ways and vocabulary, was scary, even if they were merely asking for an honest day's work. Except for a number of harborside taverns or alehouses, no shop or trade would hire them. Some former tenant farmers returned to their homes in an attempt to readapt to their former life, but few succeeded. So the majority of them returned to the harbors. If no other options were available, men reluctantly reupped onto naval and merchant ships, hoping this time their promised wages would materialize. Men became further disillusioned and vengeful concerning their lot in life for having to make this decision. This cycle would recur through the coming centuries of continual war.

For Elizabeth I, men were always needed aboard her naval fleet, and not just to confront enemies in the Caribbean Sea. She had a pirate closer to England who was a constant thorn in her side: an

Irish chieftain, Grania ni Mhaille, better known as Grace O'Malley. She was born in Ireland (circa 1530) during the Irish clan wars and England's push to occupy Ireland before Catholic Spain could get a foothold so close to Protestant England. Grace was the daughter of Owen O'Malley, chieftain of a mighty seafaring warrior clan whose territory covered the western coast of Ireland.

The O'Malley clan not only boasted huge herds of cattle, but unlike other clans who sailed close to the coastline, they ventured afar, trading with France and Spain. Upon her father's death Grace became chieftain. By creating a stranglehold on Irish commerce, England hoped Ireland would become submissive and surrender to its rule. To that end England prohibited any Gaelic clans or any nonresidents to trade in Galway, a major trading center for Ireland and England. Refusing to comply, Grace began pirating any ships outside Galway Harbor, considering them all fair game and forcing Elizabeth to divert much of her navy and military to deal with this female pirate upstart. On September 6, 1593, after many turbulent years of fighting, Grace O'Malley and Queen Elizabeth met in a private audience and agreed on a truce to curtail Grace's pirating activities.

Besides fighting Grace O'Malley so close to home and patrolling the Spanish Main, experienced sailors were needed in newly discovered countries recently opened to English trade and exploration. Trade routes abounded to India, Asia, Africa, and Madagascar, continuing along to the Middle East, most prominently to Persia (present-day Iran). In addition to the African slave trade, called "black gold" or "black ivory," one of the biggest enterprises of the English empire was the establishment of the East India Company.

Officially founded in 1600, it was financed by English businessmen and the private coffers of the English crown. The East India Company became so vital to English commerce that the company was housed in an army garrison in the city of Calcutta, India, for the protection of its employees, ships, and cargo.

The wars in Western Europe continued to allow pirates and privateers to take advantage of the less-fortified holding and commercial shipping of every country. Privateers, sailing with the protection of their nation's letter of marque and under its flag, had free rein to attack any and all enemy cities or shipping. There were strings attached, however, for the licensed privateers. Governments directly or through appointed officials received a licensing fee, a percentage of all plunder, and—perhaps most important—an additional free navy fighting their enemy.

With treaties being broken every few years, war became a never-ending cycle with ever-changing alliances affecting every man, woman, and child. Each war and treaty built up further animosity between countries. The list below represents just a fraction of the bloody conflicts raging from the sixteenth to eighteenth centuries:

- The War of the Portuguese Succession (1580–1583): Philip of Spain crowned king of Portugal. France, England, and Portuguese loyalists vs. Spain and Philip's loyalists.
- The Anglo-Spanish War (1585–1604): France, England, and Portuguese loyalists vs. Spain, Portugal, and the French Catholic League.
- The Dutch-Portuguese War (1602–1661): Dutch Republic and England vs. Portugal.
- The Anglo-French War (1627–1629): England vs. France.
- First Anglo-Dutch War (1652–1654): Commonwealth of England vs. Dutch Republic.
- The Nine Years' War (1688–1697): England, Dutch Republic, Holy Roman Empire, Spanish Empire, Duchy of Savoy, Swedish Empire, and Scotland vs. France and English Jacobites.
- The War of the Spanish Succession (1701–1714): England, Holy Roman Empire, Italy, Germany, Austria, and Dutch

Republic vs. France and Spain. Considered by many the first world war of the modern era, it is also viewed as the war that exponentially increased pirate activity.

The War of the Spanish Succession was rooted in the death of King Charles II of Spain. He died in 1700 without an heir to the throne. In his will Charles gave the crown of Spain to the French prince Philip of Anjou. King Louis XIV of France, Philip's grandfather, immediately acknowledged him as king of Spain, and declared that now France and Spain would become a united front. Because France's power was already considered too great a threat, other countries formed the Grand Alliance.

Their aim was to prevent France from acquiring Spain and to place the Hapsburg archduke Charles of Austria on the Spanish throne. The war broke out in 1701. In 1711, with the bloody conflict still raging, Emperor Joseph I of Austria died. His rightful successor for emperor of the Holy Roman Empire was Charles of Austria. This shocked and scared the other countries in the Grand Alliance.

They clearly understood that Charles would be a greater threat to them all if he controlled Spain and Austria, than if Philip became king of Spain. With this new and greater threat looming before the Grand Alliance, a shrewd King Louis XIV brokered an acceptable peace. The Treaty of Utrecht in 1713 placed Philip V on the throne of Spain with the condition that France and Spain would never unite. As part of the peace terms, England received Gibraltar, Newfoundland, Nova Scotia, the American Hudson Bay territories, and a monopoly on the slave trade in Latin America. Now officially the emperor of the Holy Roman Empire, Charles of Austria finally agreed in 1714 not to pursue the throne of Spain, and he signed the Peace of Rastatt, agreeing to all the treaty's terms.

With the Great War over, former sailors and seamen from every country watched as wealth from the Spanish Main and exotic countries beyond once again flowed freely to ports in ever-increasing numbers. As they had done numerous times in the past, each country's treasury stated that it had little to no monies to pay the wages promised to enlisted men. Decommissioned sailors as well as unemployed seamen were left to fend for themselves. Knowing they would never receive what was legally their due, an attitude of "What do I have to lose?" swept like a fever through the former ranks. Their options were starve to death, beg for scraps, turn to the criminal underground, or go to sea as a pirate. Already familiar with ship life, the vast majority decided to take a chance on piracy. With a few exceptions, the majority of pirates wished to literally "sail under the radar." Their goal was simple: steal enough wealth to sustain themselves, return to land unrecognizable, and live out a comfortable life.

And so the biggest influx of piracy began.

Chapter Two

The Allure of Pirate Life

Simply put, the hierarchal structure on a pirate ship was the extreme opposite of any nation's navy or merchant fleet. Discounting the allure of easy wealth, once again the idea of being one's own man appeared to become a reality. The opportunity to take full control of one's choice of livelihood was overwhelmingly intoxicating. To this end pirates unknowingly created one of the earliest forms of democracy.

This can be clearly seen in their complete distain of sumptuary laws. Beginning in the fourteenth century, European countries, France and England in particular, enacted these laws, which enabled the ruling classes to dictate what the middle and lower classes could legally drink, what fabrics they could wear, and even what colors of clothing they could have. Punishments ranging from monetary penalties to harsh imprisonment awaited any who dared ignore the edicts. The clergy cheerfully advanced sumptuary laws as "God-given." They preached that it was heresy to rise above one's social station in pursuit of a different livelihood or attire. Pirates brazenly flaunted their fine captured clothing whenever they went ashore, daring any local citizen to confront them.

In a more serious and enlightened representation of the democratic process, before each voyage the entire pirate compliment gathered on deck. The captain's primary job, to inform the men where he believed a prize could be found as well as the ship's destination, was reviewed. Next, the rules and regulations aboard ship, known as the ship's articles or articles of agreement, would be discussed. Having previously lived under such harsh naval rules, it was an innovative concept that allowed each man equal input on what those rules stated. Each ship's articles, though often similar in content, were unique.

When in agreement the men, including the captain, would sign the document along the borders, making sure no one signed after the last written line. This denoted to one and all that no one aboard held authority over the next man. With great ceremonial pomp, bearing either a Bible or a boarding axe, everyone swore a pledge to uphold the articles. Often the last step of the ceremony was to pass around a jug of rum mixed with gunpowder to seal the oath.

These were no mere guidelines. If any rules were broken, the perpetrator would be dealt with swiftly and cruelly. The ultimate punishment, marooning, was implemented for what they considered the most heinous of crimes: killing a shipmate in cold blood or stealing from a shipmate or the entire crew. The guilty party would be forced naked onto a deserted island, some actually mere sandbars, at low tide. If the crew felt generous, they would let the accused remain clothed for minimal protection against the unforgiving sun. Given only a small jug of water or rum, a flintlock pistol with one gunpowder cartridge and one ball, and perhaps a hardtack biscuit, his fate was sealed. If he was too cowardly to commit suicide, a combination of dehydration, heat stroke, starvation, sun poisoning, and insanity eventually did the job.

A similar concept found in every ship's articles was the pirate's own form of early workman's compensation. Essentially the crew took care of their wounded mates. In every recovered document, a list of financial compensation is recorded. The most common coin in distribution at that time was the Spanish piece of eight. It weighed one ounce of silver and was valued as one dollar. A monetary value was placed on each specific injury. Like insurance contract riders of today, the amounts varied from ship to ship. They were spelled out in a very matter-of-fact declaration: A loss of a right arm might be 600 pieces of eight; a left arm or right leg, 500 pieces of eight; a left leg, 400 pieces of eight; any finger or either eye, 100 pieces of eight.

One example is the agreement that Captain George Lowther and his crew signed before their ship *Delivery* departed to hunt treasure in 1720. The articles read as follows:

I.   The Captain is to have two full Shares; the Master is to have one Share and a half; the Doctor, Mate, Gunner, and Boatswain, one Share and a quarter.

II. He that shall be found guilty of taking up an unlawful Weapon on board the Privateer, or any Prize, by us taken, so as to strike or abuse one another, in any regard, shall suffer what Punishment the Captain and the Majority of the Company shall think fit.

III. He that shall be found Guilty of Cowardice, in the Time of Engagement, shall suffer what Punishment the Captain and Majority shall think fit.

IV. If any Gold, Jewels, Silver, & Coin be found on board of any Prize or Prizes, to the value of a Piece of Eight, and the Finder do not deliver it to the Quarter-Master in the Space of 24 Hours, shall suffer what Punishment the Captain and Majority shall think fit.

V.   He that is found Guilty of Gaming, or Defrauding another to the Value of a Shilling, shall suffer what Punishment the Captain and the Majority of the Company shall think fit.

VI. He that shall have Misfortune to lose a Limb, in Time of Engagement, shall have the Sum of one hundred and fifty pounds Sterling, and remain with the Company as long as he shall think fit.

VII. Good Quarters to be given when call'd for.

VIII. He that see a Sail first, shall have the best Pistol, or Small-Arm on board her.

Another difference among naval, merchant, and pirate ships was the authoritative position of the captain and quartermaster. As stated earlier, naval captains were considered above the law in their dealings with crew. On a pirate vessel, except for very few exceptions, such as Blackbeard's ship, the captain who began any voyage served as leader only at the whim of his crewmates. Men who turned to piracy would never again allow anyone to wield that much power over them.

The captain's main job was to find treasure and strategically know how to acquire it with as little loss as possible to man and ship. A majority vote of the entire compliment could instantly remove a man from the captaincy. There are numerous accounts of dissatisfied pirates who overthrew their original leader and appointed someone from within their ranks. Because a vote would disrupt battle preparations, the only time a captain was immune was ten minutes before a fight. If any outcome was not to a crew's liking, the captain could be killed outright or thrown overboard to take his chances. The captain didn't even have the luxury of exclusively bunking in the captain's cabin. Anyone, at any time, could use those quarters, demanding to sleep on the captain's bed.

The quartermaster oversaw the daily running of the ship and ensured adherence to the rules. Elected by the crew, he held the true authority. He had judicial authority to dole out punishment for any minor offense that occurred. For a serious offense, he became the trial judge while the captain and crew voted as jurors.

After a battle the quartermaster's major responsibility was to accumulate and sort the plunder. Laying all items out on deck for all to see, he would set aside items needed to maintain the smooth operation of the ship. Next, he would decide what could bring a good price at a friendly port. Once done with this initial sorting, he carefully watched each man take only his rightful share. In port the quartermaster dealt with not only shopkeepers, but also government officials who came aboard to collect, as protection money, their percentage for allowing the pirates a safe harbor.

The navigator, also called the sea artist or pilot, was of crucial importance on any treasure voyage. He was the professional who understood the science of the stars and how to steer a course by them. In a time when few knew how to read and write, he was literate and knowledgeable in mathematics, plotting latitude, and the crude fundamentals of chart making and drawing.

The third most sought-after man was a surgeon, also known as a barber-surgeon, as he studied for both professions. Nicknamed "Sawbones," for obvious reasons, his knowledge of local herbs and medicines, some acquired from the newly discovered international trade routes, made him indispensable. If a ship's manifest had no surgeon, the carpenter would step into that role. The tools of both professions were frighteningly similar.

Not every member of a crew served as a willing participant. As in the navy and merchant fleets, with death and disease a constant, even pirate vessels needed to replace men while sailing thousands of miles from land.

Testimonies from survivors state that once aboard a captured ship, merchant or passenger, pirates immediately sought out the professional they required. These men became so vital to the welfare of a pirate ship, it was not uncommon to threaten torture and murder to an entire ship's compliment if the sought-after individual did not step forward. If no one did, a man was randomly picked from the circle of captives and tortured until someone stepped forward.

Once they acquired the professional needed, the pirates would inquire whether any man desired to join their pirating adventures.

Amoral captains seemed surprised when a large number of their crews readily accepted the offer. Encouraged, the crew would be asked to reveal the true nature of a captain's dealings with his men. If the crew had been ill-treated, pirates would distribute their own form of justice upon him befitting the crimes he had inflicted. Often, with all the abuse they had personally received still fresh in their minds, pirates subsequently tortured the present captain for personal revenge. This reasoning partially explains some of the most brutal tortures pirates enacted on merchant captains. If, as in the case of Captain William Snelgrave, whose ship was taken in 1719, the crew vouched that the captain had dealt fairly with his men, pirates generally allowed him to live. Any additional crew the pirates required to fill their sailing compliment simply accepted their fate at gunpoint.

The practice of grabbing innocent men became so prevalent that newspapers and broadsheets, which previously announced the departure or arrival dates of a ship, began to print the names of men who departed on legitimate sailing journeys and were forced mid-voyage to join a pirate crew.

In 1704 the *Boston News-Letter*, the first newspaper in the Massachusetts Bay area, became the first paper to institute this practice. This notice became critical to the lives of those men. When a pirate ship was captured and crews sent to trial, the newspaper notice that bore evidence of forced piracy would be used in court to support a man's claim of innocence. Men forced into piracy became so prevalent that the other colonial newspapers began to print a "forced notice" column as well. Unfortunately this did not always save someone from the hangman's noose.

Though most pirates were in their mid-20s, trial records show the age span to have stretched from 17 to 50. The demands of working a ship were rigorous; agility and stamina were a must in order to remain alive. For example, imagine being hundreds of feet above sea level on a rolling ship, balancing on a mere "foot rope," leaning over the wooden yard (a horizontal spar on the mast), and adjusting hundreds of yards of sewn canvas sail weighing tons. A man needed the strength to work and hold on simultaneously. It was a treacherous job to pull up the canvas sail (furling) and then secure it to the yard with a series of ropes.

In contrast to the harsh duties of the navy or merchant fleet, daily life on a pirate ship was typically unstructured. The maintenance of most ships was kept to the bare minimum, just enough to keep the vessel afloat. When capturing a ship, besides forcing men to join their crew, it became typical for pirates to take over the better-maintained vessel, rename it, and claim it as their own. If pirates were in a generous mood and decided not to torture or kill all their captives, they might allow the survivors to sail off in the pirates' discarded ship. Allowing survivors to reach a harbor helped publicize a pirate captain or ship's deeds. If it brought terror to their name, fewer ships might resist being boarded, with fewer casualties on both sides.

Other times, a captured ship would be added to create a fleet. When that occurred the pirate captain put forth a candidate and the entire crew voted whether they wanted the man to captain the additional ship. This ploy provided them with a better chance of success during a battle.

With this practice being commonplace, most of the infamous pirate captains that we know of today were, at some point, known to each other as crewmates. Captain Benjamin Hornigold (a.k.a. Hornygold), who sailed the Main and West Indies from 1713 to 1719, is a fine example. With his fierce reputation and success at capturing prizes, many men willingly signed on to his crew. One such man was a young Edward Teach (a.k.a. Thatch), better known today as Blackbeard. Showing himself to be an excellent marksman and utterly ruthless, Teach was voted the captain of the captured French ship the *Concord*. He sailed as part of Hornigold's fleet until he branched out on his own, changing his name and persona.

This familiarity among various pirate vessels led to more than just full rosters. These men, who sailed across thousands of miles of

A buccaneer.
CREDIT: ALFRED R. WAUD, C. 1860

ocean, gathered in friendly ports. Besides the usual drinking, eating, and whoring, they exchanged information regarding the latest wars or treaties, the size of military forces in specific areas, ripe targets, and the possibility of various fleets merging into one devastating force.

While the captain and navigator coordinated the ship's destination, the men spent their time doing anything they desired with no consequences to their person. Different games of chance, within the betting rules of each ship, could be going on in any section of the ship. Though the cook on board prepared set meals, when food became plentiful aboard, the men had the freedom to eat whenever hungry on whatever was available, a luxury for men used to meager rations.

Drinking as much as they desired became one of the favored pastimes. Drunken men lay about anywhere they chose, with men working the lines merely stepping over the unconscious bodies. The downside of this uncontrolled drunkenness arose whenever crews became too drunk to defend themselves during a battle with a legal privateer or naval ship of the line.

We know of a number of these scenarios. One of the most famous drunken captures is of the pirates Mary Read, Anne Bonny, and Calico Jack Rackham. When government-mandated privateer Captain Jonathan Barnet's ship approached Rackham's ship, the *William*, his crew was too inebriated to engage in a fight. The two pirate women alone faced Barnet's men, cutlasses at the ready. With no help from the rest of the pirates, Bonny and Read fought to no avail. The entire crew was rounded up and sent to trial.

It was not unusual for a portion of a captured prize to be weaponry. When claiming a share of the booty, any man had the right to claim a confiscated cutlass or flintlock. These became his personal weapons. One unwritten rule on a ship was that all weapons be "at the ready." No matter how a man chose to spend his downtime, his flintlock had to be in firing readiness. Firearms, susceptible to rusting from the salty sea air and water, were placed below, within easy reach of the main deck. Unlike the practice on naval ships, spare cutlasses were stored in an open container, usually a barrel, for quick access.

A type of communal vengeance permeated the pirate communities. Besides having a penchant for torture and blood spilling, pirates had a complex sense of brotherhood and loyalty to their own kind, even if they were not personally acquainted with each other. After capturing a ship sailing from Boston, Blackbeard demanded to know if it was true that pirates in the Boston gaol had been executed. On receiving an affirmative answer, he promptly burnt the captured ship and told survivors he would burn any Bostonian ships he encountered for killing "his brothers."

In July of 1717, a ship captain from Boston, Thomas Fox, was captured by pirates and made to deliver a threat directly to the city, stating that they would kill every person they captured that hailed from New England if Boston dared execute another pirate.

When pirates met by chance in the middle of the ocean, cannon shots were exchanged until the sight of the Jolly Roger confirmed their true identities. Greetings would be sent and the crews met face to face to party and swap news.

The tales of extreme wealth that could be stolen were by no means exaggerated. By 1530 Spain had laid claim to an area larger than Western Europe, stretching from the islands bordering the Caribbean Sea to the Gulf of Mexico. The amount of wealth in the form of gold, silver, diamonds, rubies, and emeralds extracted from Mexico and Central and South America was staggering. Spain continually expanded its mining operations, using enslaved natives and blacks to extract the precious ores and gems no matter the cost to human lives.

The royal Spanish court counted on treasure ships to finance its ambitions of conquest. In the early months individual ships loaded down with cargo, holds so full the ships rode low in the water, set sail on prearranged dates, heading for the official treasury in Seville. They were prime targets, and pirates took full advantage of their inexperience. To help quell the tide of pirate attacks, Spain sent out treasure fleets, comprising two to three ships accompanied by armed vessels as escort. But that only deterred a few less ambitious souls.

It did not take long for an experienced pirate navigator to understand the weather patterns of the area. If he was lucky, he had obtained detailed sea charts from captured ships. These indicated hidden sandbars, sharp reefs, and rock outcroppings, as well as which direction the strong Gulf Stream currents flowed. Any of those threats could sink a ship within minutes. With a crude understanding of drawing, the navigator could compile his own sea charts.

The seasonal weather patterns had to be understood as quickly as possible to determine the best areas for attack. During the winter and fall, treasure ships left the Caribbean Islands or South America. The Leeward Islands of the West Indies, South America, and the European trade routes became prime hunting grounds. Supply ships loaded with goods from Europe arrived simultaneously. During the spring and summer months, pirates hunted near the Windward Islands of the West Indies and up the coast of Florida, the Carolinas, New York, and New England, to Newfoundland. If they weren't attacking cities or ships, pirates either traded or sold goods that they had stolen, refitted their ships, or enjoyed time in a friendly port.

The hurricane season, which runs from the summer to the early fall, was the most dangerous time in the Caribbean. Tropical storms to fierce hurricanes materialized with little to no warning. Knowledgeable crews tried to be in safe harbors or out of the region during that time of year.

But the Spanish Main was not the only geographic destination pirates of every nation went searching for treasure. By the late seventeenth century, the Sweet Trade, as it was called, stretched internationally. Ships sailed around the Cape of Good Hope, rounding South Africa on their way to Madagascar, the Red Sea countries, Asia, and countries bordering the Indian Ocean. They preyed on all ships thought to possibly yield a prize, not even caring if it was a religious pilgrim fleet on its way to or from Mecca. If a pirate or privateering ship was lucky enough to find a prize in those waters, a share might be as much as £1,000 sterling ($500,000), which is the amount each crewmate sailing with Henry Every received during only one expedition. It is no wonder boys and men took their chances against the elements, starvation, disease, and death or capture for even one prize.

CHAPTER THREE

Politics, Economics, and the Pirate Round

WHILE WARS RAGED IN THE SEVENTEENTH CENTURY FAR ACROSS the ocean, colonists in America were prospering in their business pursuits. With England concentrating on its internal power struggles, it unknowingly allowed the American colonists more control over their lives and laws than any of its other colonial holdings, far more than those in the Caribbean.

New England shipbuilding thrived, and merchant fleets shipped colonial exports not only to England, but, during the lull in fighting, to other countries, providing the colonies a constant flow of monetary prosperity. But during wartime the ships heading to England had to sail past waiting Dutch and French privateers, as well as pirates from Belgium and the Netherlands.

During the many wars, as loyal subjects of the Crown, the majority of merchant ships from the New England area—Connecticut, Maine, Massachusetts, New Hampshire, Rhode Island, and Vermont—acquired letters of marque from their colonial governors, and set out as privateers attacking enemy merchant ships and blockading enemy ports in the West Indies.

Once England's internal struggles ended and King Charles II ascended the throne, he and his administrators turned their attention back to the colonies. England desperately required a constant flow of money, not only to finance its continual wars efforts, but also to bolster its flagging commercial economy. They turned to the colonies for the solution to their financial problem by placing, in the view of the colonists, an economic stranglehold on commerce.

Beginning in 1647, Parliament enacted a series of laws called the Navigational Acts to tighten its grip once again on the flow of goods and money. Simply put, these acts stated that all goods, manufactured or grown in the colonies, had to be exported exclusively on English ships manned only by English crews. Any imported items, anything not directly manufactured in England, had to go through the port of London. After being itemized and taxed, the cargo had to be loaded onto an English ship before sailing to North America. Imported items included cod, herring, fish oil, and all whale products.

A few items that these laws regulated for export from the colonies included ironworks, leather goods, tobacco, cotton, beaver and deer skins, and wood (for ship masts), which not only affected the northern colonies, but the southern ones as well. This was in part a deliberate attempt to not only use the colonies to exclusively help England financially, but also to provoke the Dutch. Since Dutch ships had been exporting colonial goods more cheaply, Parliament saw this as a further opportunity to make England the supreme power in international trade.

Subsequent renewals and amendments to the acts, restricting more trade, were passed by Parliament in the years 1651, 1660, 1663, 1673, and 1696. Each renewal date closed another loophole in the acts and increased taxes for the colonists. The acts listed all the items that could be marketed or manufactured only in England. These restrictions created a bitter resentment. The colonists still considered themselves English subjects. They could not comprehend why they could not use their own ships and crews. Worse still, it restricted them from selling the goods wherever they wished for a higher price than they might receive from English merchants.

English products shipped to North America became so limited, and proved to be so expensive, colonists felt that they had no recourse but to illegally, in the eyes of the mother country, purchase items cheaper from other countries. With resentment over the lack of free-flowing commerce, colonists began to rile against England's interference, which inadvertently pushed many colonists to become avid supporters of piracy and smuggling.

It became painfully obvious to colonial businessmen that Parliament's representatives had now degraded them into the category of mere money-producing servants to the Crown, and no longer considered them true Englishmen with the same rights.

This view became gut-wrenchingly clear when they learned of Lord Chatham's speech in Parliament. He stated, "The British Colonists in North America have no right to manufacture so much as a nail for a horse shoe," arguing against the colonies beginning to manufacture items at home that they previously had purchased directly from England. And it stung mightily when one Lord Sheffield stated, "The only use of American colonies is the monopoly of their consumption and the carriage of their produce [to England]." These laws in fact did the direct opposite by creating a flood of pirates.

The obvious distain and debilitating laws that England continued to impose on the colonies broadened New England's view concerning the graying lines among pirates, smugglers, and privateers. A growing number of governors issued letters of marque for their colonists, in part to advance their own financial gains. It was not unusual for these pro-privateering governors to provide the ship as well for their hunting endeavors.

For a majority of pirates, the motive for "going on the account" was simple. They dreamed of acquiring as much wealth as possible, being free of any government rules, safely owning land, and starting families. Many men achieved their dream by settling on the islands of

New Providence (Nassau, the Bahamas) or Madagascar and marrying natives. Madagascar is located in the western Indian Ocean, 266 miles east of South Africa, across from Mozambique. Few luxuries were available on the remote island for these men, who were used to certain commodities. For New England privateers a new market for colonial goods opened as ships sailed to Madagascar and India. This new market route became known as the Pirate Round.

The men of the Pirate Round sailed out of a dozen ports, the largest of these being Newport, Boston, Philadelphia, and New York. The route covered a staggering 22,000 miles of tough oceangoing. The ships were loaded with all types of cargo directly manufactured or grown in the colonies. With such a long ocean voyage, the ships landed at the pirate-controlled islands of New Providence and Madagascar, sold part of their cargo, and restocked. From there they sailed past the treacherous waters of Cape Hope, Africa, trading or attacking across the Red Sea, Persian Gulf, the Coast of Malabar in India, West Africa, and the Asian continent. The ships would load their hulls with stolen goods and foreign trade items, some not seen before in the colonies, such as tie-dyed silks, spices, embroideries, silver and gold jewelry, uncut diamonds, incense, ivory, indigo, tea, muslin, calico cloth, and African slaves.

On the journey back to North America, crews were constantly on the lookout for additional prey from which to acquire even more booty. Once they arrived in North American waters, they sold these items throughout the thirteen colonies.

For pirates and privateers, "no prey, no pay" was an accurate statement. Wages weren't always promised to privateering crews before a ship set sail. Even if they were, it became obvious that after an unsuccessful trip there was no money for wages. Privateering and piracy were both a commission-only vocation, but privateers had the slight advantage of officiality tacked onto their acts.

Though the governors of Massachusetts and Pennsylvania were known to be big supporters of privateers, for a good half century every honest government official outside of New England considered Rhode Island the "chief refuge of pyrates." The statement was quite factual. Businessmen constructed more warehouses on the docks to accommodate the fact that Rhode Island had become a huge clearinghouse for captured treasure. Additionally, the colony boasted a safe harbor to refit all types of pirate vessels. Rhode Island also had the dubious reputation for the highest number of acquittals for men brought to trial on charges of piracy.

—✦—

French, Spanish, or Dutch pirates weren't the first men to plunder the New England area. Historians agree that Dixie Bull (a.k.a. Dixey Bull) has the distinct honor of being the first recorded pirate to attack shipping ventures along New England waters.

Bull arrived in the New World from London in 1631. Being from a respectable family, he had been granted land in York, Maine, from one Sir Ferdinando Gorges. Bull originally chose the life of a beaver trapper and freely bartered with colonists and Indians. From historical journals we know that he was well known among colonists and Indians from Mount Desert Island to the Piscataqua River (a tidal river between Maine and New Hampshire).

But a fateful encounter changed his destiny. In June 1632, while trading along the Penobscot River, he was attacked by a roving band of French pirates. At gunpoint they took not only his entire stock, but also his shallop (a small sailboat), leaving him destitute. Try as he might, Bull was unable to obtain any legal assistance from the local government for any monetary compensation.

Desperate and driven by revenge, he convinced fifteen Englishmen to join him on his newly acquired boat. They drew up a crude version of ship's articles and set sail. During the summer months they hunted the New England coast for any French ship they could engage in battle. Since at this particular time England was at war with France, the colonists thought nothing of his exploits, but viewed them simply as those of a privateer. Bull's crew continued their quest until they realized their already meager food supplies had dwindled to nothing.

Starvation and a thirst for revenge can do much to the soul of a man. For Bull, the only means of survival that he could imagine had him turn on his countrymen. That one thought, converted into action, turned him in the eyes of the colonial laws and his former neighbors into a pirate.

He began by attacking small colonial trading vessels and forcing some of the men into piracy. After that Bull grew braver. Sailing to the trading post at Pemaquid Harbor (Bristol, Maine), the pirates looted the settlement and ships in the harbor. The stolen goods had an estimated value of £500 ($250,000). As shots were fired during this encounter, Bull's second-in-command was killed. Since they had never been in a battle where one of them had died, this unnerved the crew.

Not too long afterward they captured a ship manned by Captain Anthony Dicks of Salem. At his crew's insistence, Bull tried to persuade Captain Dicks to help navigate their pirate vessel to Virginia, a known safe haven. Though Captain Dicks refused their demand, Bull and crew allowed him to safely sail away. Since a guaranteed safe haven was not within their grasp, Bull and his men continued to prey on English colonial trade ships and settlements.

Captain Walter Neal, the military officer of the Piscataqua (Portsmouth, New Hampshire) militia, sent a dispatch to the governor of Massachusetts, John Winthrop, outlining the incident and asking for help in eradicating the pirate.

In late November the governor dispatched an armed vessel of twenty men to meet the forty armed volunteers and several vessels Captain Neal had rallied to hunt Bull. But the weather was not in their favor. The ships became stormbound for three weeks, offering Bull and his crew ample time to execute their escape. Nevertheless, once able to sail, Neal's expedition spent two long winter months in a fruitless search before giving up and returning to their harbor.

It wasn't until the early days of February 1633 that three men who had deserted Bull's ship after the disastrous settlement shootout returned to their homes. Upon questioning they insisted that Bull had decided to side with the French. Governor Winthrop wrote in his journal some two years later that he also believed Bull eventually sided with the French.

However, this is not the opinion of one Captain Roger Clap of Dorchester, Massachusetts. In his printed memoirs of 1731, Captain Clap writes that he had a conversation with the selfsame Captain Dicks who had been captured by Bull. According to Captain Dicks, upon his refusal to pilot them to Virginia, "these men fled eastward, Bull himself got into England; but God destroyed this wretched man. Thus the Lord saved us at this time, from their wicked Device against us."

Dixie Bull's fame as "the Dread Pirate" of his time soon turned into a series of ballads. Two that have survived are "The Story of Dixie Bull" and "The Slaying of Dixie Bull." The latter, the most famous of them all, recounts a detailed sword fight between Dixie Bull and one Daniel Curtis, a fisherman from Pemaquid who by killing Bull saves the town.

Chapter Four

John Rhoades, Jurriaen Aernouts, and Peter Roderigo

In the early years of the seventeenth century, the Dutch, their nation officially known as the Republic of the Seven United Netherlands, dominated the sea and trade routes. In 1602 the Republic of the Seven United Netherlands charted the newly formed Dutch East India Company to explore the rivers and bays of North America in search of a direct passage to the Indies (Southeast Asia).

The company was mandated to claim any uncharted areas that England and Spain had not already settled. Dutch sailors traveled up and down the eastern seaboard and planted their flag on the land from the Delmarva Peninsula (Delaware and portions of Maryland and Virginia) to southwestern Cape Cod (Massachusetts) and the entire states of New York, New Jersey, and Connecticut, with a few small outpost forts in Pennsylvania and Rhode Island. And in close proximity were the French-held islands of St. Pierre, Miquelon, and Langlade, a mere twelve miles off of Newfoundland, and situated nine hundred miles northeast of New York.

With the colonial settlements of England, the Netherlands, and France in such close proximity, these three countries engaged in a series of never-ending wars, each hoping to claim the rich lands and waterways exclusively for their sovereigns.

In the summer of 1674, John Rhoades, a captain hailing from Boston, found himself unemployed and living in the Dutch-controlled city of New York in the providence of New Netherlands. There he met Captain Jurriaen Aernouts of the Dutch privateering frigate *Flying Horse*. Willem Kerckrinck, the governor of the island of Curacao (southern Caribbean Sea) in the Netherland Antilles, had sent Aernouts to attack and plunder their English and French enemies in North America.

When his ship arrived in New York Harbor, Captain Aernouts was informed that the Third Anglo-Dutch War had ended with the ratification of the Treaty of Westminster on March 5, 1674. With England and the Netherlands now allies, it became illegal through his privateering letter of marque to prey on any English ships. However, the Netherlands was still at war with France. Captain Aernouts decided to sail north and prey on the French fishing settlements along the gulf of the St. Lawrence River (the Great Lakes area).

While Captain Aernouts resupplied his ship and signed on recruits, Captain Rhoades impressed him with his vast coastal knowledge of the French colonies. Rhoades convinced him that the defenses of the French fort were inadequate, and that with his knowledge of the coastal waterways, the *Flying Horse* could easily conquer the French-held beaver-rich trade country.

Captain Aernouts put the endeavor to his officers and crew. With their approval Rhoades signed onto the ship as their navigator and swore his allegiance to Prince William of Orange, of the Netherlands. The *Flying Horse* landed at Pentagoet (Castine, Maine) on August 1, 1674. After a two-hour battle, the French fort, manned by only thirty men, surrendered, and the fort commander was taken as a hostage. Rhoades soon discovered that the fort commander, one Jacques de Chambly, was also the governor of Acadia (Eastern Quebec, Maine to the Kennebec River in west-central Maine). The

Dutch demanded a ransom of one thousand beaver pelts for his release. Unable to acquire that large number of pelts to pay the ransom, the governor remained a hostage.

Rhoades navigated the ship safely eastward to the Bay of Fundy, situated between New Brunswick and Nova Scotia. They captured every trading post and French fort as far as the St. John River, including Fort Jemseg (New Brunswick, Quebec). Captain Aernouts claimed the entire Acadia territory, now a Dutch conquest of war, which he renamed New Holland. At each new area captured, Aernouts buried a bottle containing a copy of his privateering commission along with a statement of his legal conquest. After the French accepted defeat, the Dutch released Jacques de Chambly. The *Flying Horse* remained in the area for a month to ensure that no one attempted to recapture the territory.

With their ship heavy with plunder, they sailed back to Boston in late September of 1674. Cleverly diplomatic, Aernouts applied to Governor John Leverett of Massachusetts for permission to remain in Boston Harbor to refit his ship and dispose of their goods. Governor Leverett not only granted him permission, but the colony of Massachusetts purchased all the cannons the Dutch had taken from the French forts. Boston merchants eagerly bid on the rest of the items they had pillaged.

Massachusetts fur traders and merchants had previously paid the French for the privilege of trapping and trading with the Indians in the French-controlled area of Acadia. Edward Hilliard, William Waldron, and George Manning approached Captain Aernouts with the same proposition. He refused them, stating that the commodities in the territory would be available only to Dutch citizens. With their histories of noncompliance, believing they would not be caught, these three men disregarded the decree and sailed north to continue their hunting and trading.

By November Captain Aernouts was ready to return to Curacao. Before departing he promoted John Rhoades, Peter Roderigo, and Cornelius Andreson to captains. And together with John Williams, who signed onto the expeditionary force, Aernouts granted them all the authority to return to New Holland under the flag of Prince William of Orange, to trade with the Indians and keep the French from reacquiring the area until they received further instructions. Captain Roderigo purchased the vessel *Edward and Thomas*, owned by one Thomas Mitchell of Malden, Massachusetts, who joined the privateering expedition, and a shallop named the *Penobscot*, given to Cornelius Andreson to command. A shallop is a light sailboat with one or two masts with hemp canvas sails, used mainly for coastal shipping. It can carry heavy cargo in very shallow waters.

Upon returning to the Pentagoet fort in Acadia, they found it had been pillaged of all iron and other materials that could be resold. Hunting for the perpetrators, they came upon Edward Hilliard, who said he had not been aware that he was encroaching on Dutch territory; he was released. William Waldron was also apprehended. They let him retain his ship but confiscated his entire cargo. George Manning was caught in the act of trading where he had been denied access. The Dutch boarded Manning's ship, the *Philip*, owned by John Feake. In the skirmish Manning sustained minor injuries. Captain Roderigo threatened to put him ashore on an island to rot. Manning promised he would sail under Roderigo's command, if he were allowed to remain aboard the *Philip* as captain. Roderigo relented.

Before sailing back to their trading post at Machias, Washington County, Maine, they captured a small barque owned by Major Shapleigh of New Hampshire. A barque is a larger vessel than a shallop. The classification of a barque is a ship with a minimum of three masts with square-rigged sails. Usually there are different sails for the foremast (front mast closest to the bow), aft mast (after the main), and mizzen (third) mast. Searching the barque, they discovered that Major Shapleigh did not exclusively trade pelts with the Wabanaki Indian Confederacy. The Wabanaki (which means "Those Living at the Sunrise") Confederacy comprised the Malecite, Penobscot, Pennacook, MicMac, and Sokoki Indian tribes. But Captain Roderigo discovered that Major Shapleigh also brought provisions from Port Royal, Jamaica, to the French settlers situated on the St. John River. In addition to stripping him of all his cargo, they confiscated the damaging evidence of Shapleigh's French conspiracy. The Dutch nevertheless let him resume his voyage.

Hoping the Dutch fleet would be sailing to their assistance any day, the three vessels continued to sail the Acadia area, seizing English ships that had not acquired permission to trade with the Indians of the Wabanaki Indian Confederacy.

In retribution, English colonists led pirate attacks on the Dutch settlers at Machias. On March 10, 1675, a ship captained by Thomas Cole of Nantasket, Massachusetts, sailed into Machias. Discovering only four Dutchmen present at the trading post, the colonists attacked. Quickly overpowering the men, they pulled down the Dutch flag, raised their own colors, and ransacked the building. Cole ordered one of the men, Randall Judson, to be bound and left outside the shelter without food or water for four days as retribution for his resistance to surrender.

By February 1675 news of Roderigo's various attacks had reached Boston. On February 15 John Feake appeared before the governor and his magistrates, complaining that Captain Rhoades and his cohorts had illegally pirated his property. Since William Waldron and others had already signed protests concerning numerous piratical attacks, the governor had to act.

Though the Dutch considered their actions in alliance to their decree, the colonial governor considered their action that of piracy against an ally. Captain Samuel Mosely (a.k.a. Mosley) was dispatched to apprehend the Dutch fleet. Unbeknownst to Rhoades and Roderigo, though the Republic of the Seven United Netherlands was still at war with France, the English and French had signed a peace treaty. On his way to capture the Dutch fleet, Captain Mosely encountered a French ship. Convincing them to join him, Mosely outfitted the French with additional men, guns, and ammunition.

Captain Roderigo's fleet was taken by surprise. Captain Manning seized that moment to switch back his loyalties, and turned his guns on the Dutch fleet. Edward Youring, an English seaman on the *Edward and Thomas* who had been beaten by Captain Roderigo, immediately lowered the ship's mainsail, making it hard to maneuver the ship. He then hurried and lowered the Dutch flag, a sign of surrender. Being outnumbered and outmaneuvered, the Dutch surrendered. Captain Manning returned to Boston on April 2, 1675, with his prisoners. With the Dutch fleet no longer guarding New Holland, the French immediately seized the territory back, allowing the English to once again openly trade and trap with the Indians.

The Court of Assistants in Boston comprised the governor, his deputy, and appointed assistants. They all convened on April 7 and ordered the pirates to the prison at Cambridge, Massachusetts. They returned the *Philip* to John Feake and kept the other two vessels to be paid out for court expenses.

Captain John Rhoades, Captain Peter Roderigo, Captain Cornelius Andreson, and John Williams went to trial the week of May 22, 1675. Their crewmates John Thomas (a.k.a. Tomas or Tombs), Thomas Mitchell, Randall Judson, Edward Youring, Richard Tulford, Richard Fowler, Edward Uran, and Peter Grant had their day in court on May 24, 1675. At each trial, as their defense they presented the letters of marque to demonstrate the legality of their actions. Since Captain Aernouts and not Prince William of Orange had signed them, the documents were not viewed as legal. Additionally, they stated in their defense against the English pirates that Captain Thomas Cole had not only violated the Dutch territory, but also had stolen from an ally.

Thomas Mitchell, Peter Grant, and Randall Judson admitted to going ashore at Casco Bay, Maine, and stealing sheep from the farm of a Mr. Mountjoy, as they had been without provisions. John Thomas stated at trial that he was one of Captain Roderigo's crew when the ship had first sailed from Boston. John Williams stated that he had sailed out of Jamaica with a Captain Morrice but was captured by the Dutch and taken to Curacao. There he joined Captain Aernouts's privateering venture and sailed on the *Flying Horse* to Boston. When Aernouts returned to Curacao, Williams stayed and joined Captain Roderigo's crew on the *Edward and Thomas*. Thomas Mitchell stated that he lived near Malden, Massachusetts, and with Edward Uran, a fisherman from Boston, had their ship captured by Rhoades and had no other option but piracy. The Court of Assistants found them all guilty of piracy and scheduled them to hang.

The Dutch States-General interceded, complaining that their actions were legal and not piratical in nature. Petitions for pardon were sent to the court for Andreson and Roderigo. They were pardoned. The others remained in prison for months awaiting their execution.

By 1675 the Indian chief known as King Philip had declared war against the English colonists who, for the last fifty-five years, had heavily encroached on Indian territories. King Philip's War is also called America's first major Indian war. Metacom, leader of the Pokanokets tribe, received the nickname of "King Philip" from the early English settlers because of his haughty mannerisms. Ironically, it was his father, Chief Massasoit, who had helped the Plymouth Pilgrims to survive during their first winter in the New World. Events came to a head after some braves killed a few English-owned cattle that were yet again trampling the Indians' cornfields. A farmer retaliated by killing an Indian. The conflict had finally met its breaking point. This created an Indian uprising that clearly threatened to wipe out the entire Massachusetts Bay and Plymouth Bay Colonies.

In the pursuing chaos of impending war with the Indians, all executions were deferred, and the condemned men set free. Rhoades, Grant, and Judson were pardoned on the condition that they be banished from Massachusetts, never to return on pain of death. Richard Fowler returned home to his wife.

In 1676 Captain Roderigo served with Captain Joshua Scottow against the Indians in the battle at Black Point in Scarborough, Maine. Cornelius Andreson joined an independent military company commanded by Captain Samuel Mosely, the selfsame man Andreson had previously encountered while privateering. On September 12, 1675, he fought with Captain Thomas Wheeler's militia at the Battle of Bloody Brook, near Groton, Massachusetts. He left New England on October 13, 1675, and there we lose his trail.

Captain John Rhoades received a trading license from the Dutch West India Company. The license allowed him to trade in North and South America and Africa. In 1676 he sailed with Cornelius Van Steenwyk, then governor of New Holland, and twice the mayor of New York City, to Fort Pentagoet, in an attempt to finally repel the English. With three English warships against their meager fort armaments, the Dutch fell. After this crushing defeat Rhoades sailed up the Saint George River in Maine, trading and once again attacking ships. When he was easily recaptured by the English, the Dutch West India Company came to his defense, arguing he had the right to trade and defend himself if attacked. The English court allowed that he could be released to the Dutch if imprisoned in New York City. It was agreed, and on May 21, 1679, Rhoades once again found himself in a gaol. After a brief stay Rhoades was released and disappeared into history. Of the other pardoned pirates there was no further known piratical activity.

CHAPTER FIVE

Thomas Pound and Thomas Hawkins

IN 1686 THE *ROSE*, A ROYAL NAVY FRIGATE, SAILED INTO BOSTON Harbor. Aboard her sailed Thomas Pound, junior officer and ship's navigator. Along with his navigational duties, he was the naval cartographer, assigned to map out the existing coastlines of New England.

Being a naval officer, Pound was able to associate and socialize with the more prominent citizens of Boston. He quickly became a trusted friend of Sir Edmund Andros, governor of New England. Sir Andros, after his appointment in 1686 by King James II, immediately set about on the king's wishes to reduce the autonomy of the colonies. To that end Andros forced Connecticut, Massachusetts, Plymouth, Rhode Island, New York, New Hampshire, and East and West Jersey into the newly created Dominion of New England.

The very independent and proud colonies were vehemently against this move, yet had no recourse against his decree. Governor Andros also attempted to force Episcopalian worship onto the very Puritan Old South Meetinghouse in Boston. This act enraged the prominent Puritan ministers, especially Cotton Mather and his father, Increase Mather.

To make matters worse, Sir Andros strongly enforced the Navigational Acts, making enemies not only in Boston, but also in all the other port towns of the dominion.

In 1688 the "Glorious Revolution" occurred in England, in which Catholic James II was ousted by Protestant William of Orange and his Protestant wife, Mary (daughter of Catholic James II). Receiving the news in the early months of 1689, the people of Boston seized Governor Andros and his officials and immediately threw them in gaol.

Bostonians, in their built-up rage against Andros, also seized the frigate *Rose*. A frigate is a medium-size square-rigged ship with multiple guns. They dismantled her topmast and canvas sails, rendering the ship useless for any type of escape. However, Sir Andros managed to escape the Boston gaol. He was recaptured in Rhode Island on August 5 and sent back to Boston. Luckily for Sir Andros, the colonists merely packed him up and sent him back to England.

Perhaps Pound felt his close association with Andros put him in physical peril. Because it was during Governor Andros's forced return to Boston that junior officer Thomas Pound made an unusual decision, one that he chose never to explain. He decided to turn pirate.

It began on Thursday, August 8, 1689—by all trial recollections, at approximately eleven in the evening near the tidewater of Bull's Wharf in Boston, now known as Dewey Square. Pound hired Thomas Hawkins's Bermudas boat. A Bermudas boat is a two-masted, half-decked fishing boat, a design that originated in Bermuda. He asked Hawkins to take him and his friends to Nantasket (Hull, Massachusetts). Hawkins found nothing suspicious as Pound and his compatriots Thomas Johnston, Eleazar Buck, John Siccadam, Richard Griffin, and a young boy by the name of Benjamin Blake boarded his vessel with firearms.

By the time Hawkins sailed the Bermudas boat to Long Island in Boston Harbor, Pound, without explanation, ordered Hawkins to anchor until morning. Since Pound had already paid for the trip, Hawkins complied without comment. On the morning of August 9, Pound informed Hawkins that he and his friends had talked the night before and decided to go fishing instead. Hawkins hauled up anchor and sailed toward Pound's favorite fishing spots. As they neared

Lovell's Island (in Boston Harbor), a boat with five men carrying weapons came alongside. They boarded the Bermudas boat with no resistance from its passengers.

To Hawkins's chagrin, Pound introduced his friends: Daniel Lander, Samuel Watts, William Warren, Henry Dipper, and William Dunn. Pound calmly informed Captain Hawkins that they were seizing his vessel and ordered him to sail to Brewster Island. When Hawkins hesitated, Pound explained their plan to sail to the West Indies and attack the French. Hawkins agreed to take part, becoming their willing navigator. With all men in agreement, they set sail at once.

Some hours later, as they neared Brewster Island, the pirates came upon a sloop heading into port, captained by Isaac Prince from Hull, Massachusetts. With the other men hidden below deck, Hawkins hailed Captain Prince and purchased fish and barrels of water. But Price became suspicious when Hawkins kept maneuvering his ship in an evasive course, never allowing the two vessels to get close. When Prince asked Hawkins where he was headed, Captain Prince heard laughter from below deck. Hawkins lied and told Prince they were heading for Billingsgate (now Wellfleet, Massachusetts). Captain Prince commented that Hawkins was very far north of his destination. Laughing, Hawkins flippantly replied, "It's all one to me" and quickly sailed away. His comment made no sense to Prince, confirming his suspicions. After landing in Boston, Captain Prince went directly to Governor Thomas Hinckley's office to report the incident. The governor, however, brushed off Hawkins's vessel as a ship full of drunken fishermen, a situation not uncommon in those waters.

Now safely away, Hawkins sailed near Halfway Rock (between Boston and Gloucester Harbors) and spotted the fishing ketch *Mary* heading toward Boston. A fishing ketch is a two-masted ship, with the forward mast being taller. Interestingly, Philip English, who owned the *Mary*, was a successful Salem merchant who in 1683 was accused and acquitted of witchcraft. Piloting the *Mary* was Captain Allen Chard. Since Chard knew both Hawkins and Johnston, he pulled

A pirate crew's ruse for luring a merchantman.
CREDIT: UNKNOWN, C. 1896

the *Mary* alongside to greet the men, only to have his ship boarded by armed pirates. Hawkins calmly told Chard that they were taking the *Mary* as their prize. He assured Captain Chard they'd return his ship, once they acquired a better one to sail them to the West Indies. Hawkins bragged that they expected to get at least forty more men to join their adventure.

Under the watchful eye of Captain Pound and the other armed pirates, they transferred the entire crew of the *Mary* onto Hawkins's Bermudas boat and sent them on their way. Crewman John Darby of Marblehead willingly remained with the pirates. The pirates also restrained a French lad with the intention for him to be their interpreter when encountering a French ship.

Once aboard the *Mary*, Pound took stock of their weaponry. They had ample weapons at their disposal, but only two gallons of black powder for the guns and minimal ammunition. He ordered the others to immediately strip all the lead they could find aboard and melt it into bullets.

Captain Chard and his men reached Salem on August 12. Word of the incident was immediately sent to Governor Hinckley. The Salem and Marblehead militias manned a vessel and went out in search of the pirates. Despite weeks of searching, they were unsuccessful.

Meanwhile, Captain Pound set his course to Casco Bay, Falmouth, Maine. He dropped anchor some four miles from Fort Loyal. It so happened that John Darby was an acquaintance of the fort commander, Captain Silvanus Davis. Darby, with two other pirates, took the ship's longboat ashore. While the other men filled water barrels, Darby relayed a tale to Davis. He stated they had come from Cape Sable (Nova Scotia) and had been set upon by pirates who took all their provisions. Darby requested a doctor to go aboard the *Mary* since his captain had been injured in the altercation. Captain Davis sent the fort doctor to administer to the wounded fictional captain. Once aboard the *Mary*, the men attempted to cajole the doctor to become part of their crew. Refusing their offer, the doctor departed without incident, but strangely did not report the pirates to his commander.

That night seven deserters from the fort—John Hill, John Watkins, John Lords, William Neff, William Bennett, James Danell, and Richard Phipes—grabbed everything they could from the sleeping soldiers and joined the pirates. Captain Pound was thrilled about not only the additional men but also the items they brought. The ship now had a large supply of clothes, black powder, muskets, ammunition, swords, and even a small brass cannon.

Next morning Commander Davis was horrified to discover the desertion and theft. He foolishly ordered two soldiers to row out to the ketch and demand the men and items be returned. Captain Pound refused. Pound threatened to destroy the sloop that was anchored in the harbor, thus blocking any ships from entering the port. With no cannons mounted on the fort walls for defense, the *Mary* freely sailed away.

Captain Pound began to search each island on the bay for livestock. After seizing only three sheep and a calf, he and his crew sailed to Cape Cod. On August 16 they spotted the sloop *Good Speed*, captained by John Smart. After easily capturing the ship, they transferred Captain Smart and his crew onto the *Mary*. The pirates set them free to deliver a message to the authorities. When the *Mary* sailed into Boston on August 19, Captain Smart went straight to the governor's office. The message was a simple one: "They knew where the government sloop lay ready, but if she came out after them and came up with them she should find hot work for they would die every man before they would be taken."

Outraged, Governor Hinckley sent out the armed sloop *Resolution* with forty volunteers under the command of Joseph Thaxter. What made the forty regular seamen willing to serve upon the militia sloop was the unusual promise the governor put into the official records: "Those men who shall go forth in said Vessel . . . It's Ordered that they be upon usual monthly wages, and upon any casualty befalling any of the said men by loss of Limb or otherwise be maimed that meet allowance and provision be made for such." The *Resolution* had the same bad luck trying to find the pirates as the Salem and Marblehead militia.

Still on the run, Captain Pound knew he needed to restock his ship with enough provisions to sail to the West Indies. On August 27 he thought he had found the solution. The pirates came across Captain John Kent's ship, the *Merrimack*, with her full cargo. At gunpoint Captain Kent provided them with twenty half-barrels of flour, sugar, rum, and tobacco and three guns. Starting their journey to the West Indies, the *Good Speed* got caught in a stiff northeasterly gale. The ship was blown off course to Virginia. Captain Pound managed to put into the York River area for eight days. While the crew repaired the storm-damaged ship, both Pound and Hawkins went ashore. There they met two sailors, John Giddings and Edward Browne. The men had with them a black slave they had kidnapped. After speaking with

Pound and Hawkins, the two sailors decided pirating and fighting the French would be a grand adventure and joined the crew.

Luck was still with the pirates, for Giddings and Browne told them the military man-o-war ketch that was usually at the mouth of the York River had recently sunk while the other military sloop was being careened. As soon as their vessel was ready, the pirates sailed once again to the familiar waters of Massachusetts. This time they laid anchor at Tarpaulin Cove, situated on the southeast side of Nanshon Island in Martin's Vineyard Sound (renamed Martha's Vineyard). While refilling their water casks, they anchored alongside another fishing vessel. Hawkins went aboard her to see if they could overpower the crew. Deciding it too dangerous an attempt, Hawkins traded some of their sugar for a needed anchor. Hawkins also sold the black slave they had acquired to the captain, William Lord, for £12 sterling ($6,000).

Feeling a bit cocky, Captain Pound tried to capture a ketch commanded by Captain Alsop by cutting her off in Martin's Vineyard harbor. The pirates were prevented from their goal when other small ships in the harbor came to Captain Alsop's aid by blocking the *Good Speed*. With that disappointing defeat the pirates sailed back to Cape Cod.

Near Race Point (at the tip of Cape Cod), Hawkins and some of the crew went ashore to gather more provisions. At that moment Hawkins decided to desert the pirates. Perhaps he felt that, with all the plundering of local shipping and the trip to the West Indies not coming to fruition, he would leave before all aboard the *Good Speed* were captured. Trying not to alert the other men of his plan, Hawkins gave them some excuse and disappeared inland across the dunes. After walking for some time, Hawkins had a chance meeting with a well-known friend from Boston. Captain Jacobus Loper, a Portuguese whaler and oysterman, had been fishing on Cape Cod since 1665. With his ship full of oysters, Loper was sailing back to Boston that day. Hawkins signed on for the voyage back.

Hawkins made the mistake of talking very openly to Captain Loper about his adventures with Thomas Pound. Loper admonished him, warning he would be hanged for his acts. Hawkins defensively replied that it would never happen. During the entire time he had been pirating, he had killed no one. But as the ship neared Boston, Hawkins got scared. He tried to talk his old friend into concealing him. When that failed, he asked Captain Loper to sail to Salem, not Boston, to sell his oysters. Hawkins argued he could escape from Salem onto the Dutch man-o-war *Abraham Fisher*, which lay anchored outside Salem Harbor. Captain Loper knew it would be best for him and his crew if he turned Hawkins over to the authorities. Hawkins's greatest fear was realized when he sat in irons and chains in the newly constructed four-feet-thick stone gaol awaiting trial for piracy.

Meanwhile, Hawkins's desertion didn't seem to bother Pound. Since he was a navigator, Pound continued to attack and rob vessels of every size along Cape Cod. With no luck finding a ship with enough salt pork and bread for a long journey, Captain Pound sailed the *Good Speed* back to Vineyard Sound. On October 1 at Homes Hole, he spotted the exact ship he had been hoping to find.

The inclement weather had forced Captain John Picket's sloop, the *Brothers Adventure*, out of New London, Connecticut, to seek shelter. The sloop had been on its way to Boston fully loaded with cargo. Pound convinced Captain Picket to anchor alongside the *Good Speed* for easy companionship. That evening Pound and his men boarded the unsuspecting sloop. The pirates seized the entire cargo, consisting of thirty-nine barrels of salt pork and beef, seven firkins (each an eleven-gallon capacity) of butter, thirteen wheels of cheese, three barrels of Indian corn, and eight bushels of peas. At last having ample provisions for the long journey to Curacao, Captain Pound laid in at Tarpaulin Cove, waiting for the weather to turn favorable for the voyage. He believed his plan easy to accomplish. At that moment the Netherlands was at peace with England. He'd sail to the Dutch-held island, refit the *Good Speed*, and hunt French ships sailing out of the island of Martinique.

But Captain Pound did not count on one of his prey, a vessel that had successfully escaped, sailing into Martin's Vineyard harbor to rush to the local governor with the news. Governor Matthew Mayhew sent word to Governor Hinckley in Boston to warn all westbound shipping of piratical activity. On September 30 Governor Hinckley ordered Captain Samuel Pease and Lieutenant Benjamin Gallop to arm the Boston sloop *Mary* and capture the pirates with as little loss of blood as possible. Ironically, Captain Pease's sloop *Mary* was the same ship that Hawkins and Pound had previously seized from Captain Chard.

On Friday, October 4, the *Mary* sailed to the entrance of Tarpaulin Cove. A local man confirmed the pirates were indeed in the area. Raising its anchor, the *Mary* sailed south by southeast into a strong wind and soon spotted a sloop. Not sure if the ship was indeed their intended target, Captain Pease ordered the Union Jack raised onto the mainmast. Additionally, he ordered a recognition shot be fired across her bow. The militia volunteers watched as an unadorned red flag was hoisted on the *Good Speed*. Traditionally, a red flag raised by pirates meant they would serve their enemy no quarter, killing all who opposed them. Captain Pease ordered their surrender, but Pound stood on the quarterdeck, sword in hand, daring them to board the *Good Speed* and fight to the death.

A fierce gun battle ensued, with each side firing as fast as it could prime, reload, and take aim. An explosion on the *Mary* killed a number of men. Pound was shot, forcing him to go below deck. On seeing Pound leave the main deck, Captain Pease once again ordered the pirates' surrender. They refused. With the next barrage of gunfire, Captain Pease was seriously wounded. Lieutenant Gallop took command. He ordered his men to board the pirate ship. The battle turned into a bloody hand-to-hand fight. As soon as muskets were fired, the militiamen and pirates used the butt end of their weapons as clubs.

The men of the *Mary* overpowered the pirates. Surveying their victory, they discovered that five pirates lay dead. Three were from Fort Loyal: Corporal John Hill and privates, John Lords, and John Watkins. Along with Henry Dipper from Lovell's Island and John Darby, the former crewman of the *Mary*. Twelve lay wounded and two miraculously appeared unscathed.

With the weather getting worse, Lieutenant Gallop ordered his men to secure the prisoners and sail both ships toward Rhode Island. They got as far as Pocasset, Massachusetts, before the weather turned on them again. Gallop sent word to Newport, requesting doctors or surgeons. By October 11 Captain Pease felt well enough to order the expedition to return to Boston. But on the 12th Pease died of his wounds. His men buried him in Newport. On October 18 they entered Boston Harbor. It was in the Boston gaol that Thomas Pound reunited with Thomas Hawkins.

Governor Hinckley ordered a doctor to tend to the wounded pirates in order for them to be healthy enough to stand trial. As recorded by Thomas Larkin, Dr. Elisha Cooke treated the prisoners and sent a detailed bill to the colonial government for £21 sterling and 10 shillings ($10,750). The severe wounds on several men revealed the ferocity of the fight:

Thomas Pound: shot in the arm and side. He required bones removed.

Thomas Johnston: shot in the jaw. He required a section of his jawbone removed.

Eleazar Buck: seven bullet wounds in his arm.

Richard Griffin: shot in the ear with the bullet exiting his eye. He lost the eye.

Edward Browne: shot in the hand and lost his top joints.

John Giddings: numerous wounds in both arms.

Richard Phips: shot in the head, lived.

Daniel Lander: shot through the arm.

William Warren: shot in the head, lived.

John Siccadam: shot in both legs.

They all languished, shackled and chained in the gaol, until January 13, 1690. The men were tried in two groups along with other pirates who had been caught and set for trial. The charges read out were murder, felony, and piracy. After the guilty verdict was read, deputy governor Thomas Danforth ordered the January 27 execution of Thomas Hawkins, Eleazar Buck, Thomas Pound, and Thomas Johnston.

During the trial five men from the *Mary*—Benjamin Gallop, Daniel Langley, Colburn Turell, Abraham Addams, and John Paine—identified Thomas Johnston as the man who had fatally shot Captain Pease. The boy, Benjamin Blake, received a full pardon and was freed. Edward Browne was acquitted. The other pirates returned to the gaol, awaiting a ruling on their petition. During that time Richard Phipes and William Bennett died.

The sensational trials of pirates always drew large public crowds, the press, and the Puritan Reverend Cotton Mather. The famous judge and diarist Samuel Sewall traveled to Boston to attend the trial and accompanied Mather to the gaol to pray for the souls of the condemned.

Not happy with the men's sentencing, magistrate Waitstill Winthrop decided his only recourse was to obtain a reprieve for the men. He set about gathering signatures from the many prominent officials and influential families of the area who knew them.

He pointed out that a murder charge did not apply to Hawkins because he was not in the company of pirates at the time of Captain Pease's death. Mere moments before the noose tightened around

Hawkins's neck, the executioner received a reprieve order. Thomas Johnston, with no influential men or women to vouch for him, became the only pirate to hang that day.

On February 20 a ruling was announced. Thomas Hawkins, William Warren, Samuel Watts, Daniel Lander, Richard Griffin, John Siccadam, Eleazar Buck, William Dunn, William Neff, and James Danell were pardoned of all crimes. The court ordered each man to pay a fine of 20 marks (£13.6s.8p., or $6,666) to cover the costs of their imprisonment and prosecution. If the men refused to pay, their only alternative to fulfill the debt was to go up on the slave block in Virginia. The men gladly paid the 20 marks. With the exception of Hawkins, after all the other men paid their debts, no more was heard about their lives.

A separate petition had been circulating among the friends and relatives of Thomas Pound, and among the women of Boston's high society, to pardon Pound. On February 24 he received a reprieve, not a pardon, and orders to sail to England, where his fate would be determined.

On April 20, 1690, the Royal Navy frigate *Rose*, captained by John George, sailed from Nantasket with Thomas Hawkins and Thomas Pound united once again. The ship's first destination was Piscataqua. The *Rose* anchored there for a month, waiting for two vessels carrying a cargo of wooden ship masts. The three ships planned to convoy to England.

The voyage went smoothly until May 24, when the *Rose*, sailing off Cape Sable Island, Nova Scotia, encountered a privateering ship from St. Malo, France. The privateer, with thirty cannons, managed to get close to the *Rose* by deceptively flying an English flag. When it drew near enough to the *Rose*, it hoisted a French flag.

The *Rose* signaled the cargo ships to sail to a safe distance while it engaged the French. A fierce two-hour battle ensued. The *Rose* had her mizzenmast, sails, rigging, and ensign flag shot down. Amidst the rubble on deck, the *Rose* managed to severely damage the French privateer with a port broadside. When the French captain and lieutenant were killed, the privateer's crew stopped firing, turned, and sailed away. Among the dead on the main deck of the *Rose* lay Thomas Hawkins.

Thomas Pound reached Falmouth, England, on July 8, 1690. He wrote to Sir Edmund Andros, who now resided in London, recounting the events in New England and his most recent battle with the French.

In 1691 Pound published a navigational map entitled "A New Mapp of New England." It would be used consistently for the next fifty years. The only known copy is now housed in the US Library of Congress. Pound dedicated the map to his patron, Charles Gerard, Earl of Macclesfield.

Having Pound's sentence of piracy expunged, on August 5, 1690, the Earl of Macclesfield secured Pound a captaincy on the Royal Navy ship *Sallee Rose*, a frigate captured from the Moors. His ship patrolled the English Channel until February 2, 1695, when he was transferred as captain to the *Dover Pride*. His orders were to sail to the colony of Virginia and report to the new governor, Sir Edmond Andros. Pound served the Virginia colony until March 22, 1698, when he received orders to sail the *Dover Pride* back to England.

He retired to private life in 1699 and lived as a gentleman in Isleworth, Middlesex, until his death in 1703.

CHAPTER SIX

Thomas Tew and
Governor Benjamin Fletcher

THOMAS TEW WAS BORN TO A PROMINENT NEWPORT, RHODE Island, seafaring family at a time when piracy and privateering were an important industry for that colony. When pirates or privateers brought cargo ashore at Rhode Island port towns, the custom tax that would normally be sent to England from legitimate shipping did not get collected. Goods from pirate cargos were sold locally, at a substantially lower price than goods being shipped from England. The infrastructure of the colony also benefited from the "fees" issued on a pirate's plunder by the local government. These fees made it no longer necessary to collect taxes from residents. As an added bonus, Rhode Island merchants were able to sell their local products of food, lumber, liquor, leather goods, and shipbuilding repair services to all inbound pirates.

In the 1680s Tew sailed as a privateer out of Port Royal, Jamaica. He landed in 1691 on the island of Bermuda. There he purchased a share in the sloop *Amity* along with other merchants and officials of the island. William Outerbridge, a member of the Governor's Council, was a major shareholder. With so many prominent personages backing the ship's voyage, the Jamaican governor, William O'Brien, the Second Earl of Inchiquin, issued a privateering letter of marque. Having no difficulty obtaining a willing crew of sixty seasoned men, Tew took command of the *Amity*. Another privateering sloop, captained by George Drew, joined the expedition.

Besides disrupting French commercial shipping, Captain Drew had a secondary mission. The lieutenant governor of Bermuda, Isaac Richier, instructed Drew to attack and seize the French slaveholding warehouse on the island of Goree, off the coast of Senegal, Africa. Also an agent for the English Royal African Company, Richier hoped to claim the French factory, as it was called, as part of England's territory. It would afford England an even larger stake in the African slave trade. But a fierce storm blew up unexpectedly. When it finally abated a few days later, the two ships had lost sight of each other. George Drew and crew were never seen again.

It was at this point in time that Tew decided on a change in course. He gathered his men together on the deck of the *Amity* and put forth an interesting proposition. He asked them to sail as pirates to the Red Sea for their own self-interests. Captain Charles Johnson in his book, *A General History of the Robberies and Murders of the Most Notorious Pyrates*, published in 1724, summarizes Tew's alleged speech. What is interesting is that it clearly reveals the populace feeling about the way society treated the common man and his hard work.

> *That they [the ship's crew] were not ignorant of the Design with which the Governor fitted them out; the taking and destroying the French factory; that he [Tew], indeed, readily agreed to take a Commission to this end, tho' contrary to his Judgment, because it was being employ'd; but that he thought it a very injudicious Expedition, which did they succeed in, would be of no Use to the Publick, and only advantage a private Company of Men, from whom they could expect no Reward of their Bravery; that he could see nothing but Danger in the Undertaking, without the least Prospect of a Booty; that he could not suppose any Man fond*

of fighting, for fighting-sake; and few ventured their Lives, bit with some View either of particular Interest or publick Good; but here was not the least Appearance of either. Wherefore, he was of Opinion, that they should turn their Thoughts on what might better their Circumstances; and if they were so enclined, he would undertake to shape a Course which should lead them to Ease and Plenty, in which they might pass the rest of their Days. That one bold Push would do their Business, and they might return home, not only without Danger, but even with Reputation.

Captain Tew's shipmates unanimously agreed, where upon Tew asked them to nominate a quartermaster for the journey. Once done, Captain Tew changed course and sailed around the Cape of Good Hope to the Straits of Babel Mandel (also known as Bab el Mandeb), one of the narrowest points in the Red Sea. They sighted a pilgrim fleet of six ships sailing from India on their way to the port of Jiddah, near Mecca. Being miles ahead of the fleet, the first vessel was larger than the rest and loaded with tribute treasure. Sighted on her deck, along with numerous mounted cannons, stood three hundred Indian soldiers.

At first the pirates became reluctant to engage such a large vessel with that many soldiers and cannons. Tew convinced them the soldiers, though many in number, were "heathen" soldiers who had no skill to fight nor the courage to do so. His men finally agreed. The altercation was over almost before it began; the soldiers gave up quickly. Not one of Tew's crew died. After stripping the ship of its treasure, consisting of gold, silver, uncut diamonds, and other jewels, each man's share came to roughly £3,000 sterling ($1.5 million). The pirates seized so much gunpowder that, after loading the *Amity* to capacity, they dumped the excess into the sea. Tew urged his men to hunt down the other five ships for their possible treasure haul, but he was voted down. With the crew's decision made, Tew sailed the *Amity* to the island of St. Mary's (St. Marie), off Madagascar, and safety.

Twenty-four of his crewmates decided to remain on the idyllic island. The rest agreed to sail back to North America with Tew. As they sailed north on the Atlantic side of the Cape of Good Hope, the pirates seized a Dutch East Indiaman—a ship owned by the Dutch East India Company—manned by eighteen guns (cannons were called guns when mounted on a ship). During the fighting only one pirate lost his life. The Indiaman, on its way to purchase various commodities, was loaded with chests of English silver crowns. Nine of the Dutchman's crew signed on with Tew. The pirates set the rest of the Dutch sailors ashore at Soldinia Bay (near Cape Town, Africa).

Continuing on, they spied an English ship off the coast of Angola (west side of Africa) and seized it. It was a slaver carrying over 240 black men, women, and children aboard. Many of Tew's black crewmen discovered friends and relatives chained aboard the slaver. The pirates voted to return to Madagascar so they could land the freed slaves on the island. Back on Madagascar, it was discovered that the *Amity's* hull needed to be careened because of the damage caused by barnacles and Teredo worms.

Waiting for the repairs to be completed, Captain Tew took out to sea on the sloop *Liberty*, mounted with eight guns and manned by one hundred pirates. Joining his fleet was a pirate named Schoolmaster commanding the sloop *Childhood*. When not searching for prey, the two sloops spent four months surveying the coastline of Madagascar and St. Mary's, charting the shoals, currents, and water depths.

By the end of the four months, the *Amity* was fit for sea. Tew proposed to return to North America and arrange for colonial merchants to send their wares to Madagascar and St. Mary's for the comfort of the pirates who lived on the island. Since many of his crew had families back in the colonies, his men were quite agreeable. Tew planned to first return to Bermuda to pay off the shareholders of the *Amity*. A severe gale forced him to make for the safety of Newport, Rhode Island. As the plunder was piled on the dock, news of the vast fortune being unloaded spread throughout the town. The patrons of every tavern, alehouse, brothel, and inn greeted the pirates with much gaiety. Merchants from Boston, Philadelphia, and New York arrived in town eager to partake of the booty.

Captain Tew was the first of the "Red Sea Men" to make arrangements with honest merchants to engage in the Pirate Round. He convinced them that items such as beer, rum, and local goods would fetch higher prices from the men living on St. Mary's, Madagascar, and New Providence. At the same time, returning with luxury goods from India was worth the long, often torturous voyages.

When all was said and done, the share of Tew's major investor in Bermuda, William Outerbridge, paid out at £3,540 sterling ($1.77 million). Tew walked off with a share of £8,000 sterling ($4 million).

A shrewd businessman, Captain Tew frequently traveled to New York City. He met with numerous merchants, carefully disposing of portions of his seized plunder. For a percentage of their profits, he helped businessmen arrange shipments of specific goods to Madagascar. It is also mentioned that he chose to move his wife and two daughters to the city, where they enjoyed quite the social life.

Unable to obtain a personal privateering letter of marque from Rhode Island governor John Easton, Tew looked to New York's governor, Benjamin Fletcher. Under Fletcher's governorship New York became even a greater open port for pirates and privateers. In October of 1694 Captain Tew called at the governor's mansion to request a privateering commission allowing him to legally attack their French enemy along the Canadian coast.

On November 2, 1694, Governor Fletcher had his secretary, Daniel Honan, issue the letter of marque for a percentage bond of the profits. Captain Tew made the bond payment of £3,000 ($1.5 million), and the commission was countersigned and witnessed by Edward Coats, another captain who sailed the Pirate Round. Just prior, Captain Coats had personally presented Governor Fletcher with a captured prize ship, which Fletcher sold for a profit of £800 ($400,000). It was commonly known that for £100 ($50,000) paid to

Fletcher, a pirate could safely walk the streets of New York. Tew did more than that; it was not uncommon to see him ride around the city with Fletcher in the governor's carriage. As a token of his friendship, Fletcher presented Tew with a gold watch.

Though his letter of marque was to attack their French enemies, Tew made it known to all in New York that with his commission secured he intended to journey back to the Red Sea area and return to the port of New York with his booty.

Captain Tew returned to Newport, Rhode Island, in preparation for the trip. While readying the *Amity*, he was joined by three former buccaneering friends, their ships already outfitted to make a journey. The *Dolphin*, out of Philadelphia and captained by William Want, carried six guns and was manned by sixty men. Joseph Farrell, hailing from Newport, Rhode Island, captained the *Portsmouth Adventure* with six cannons and twenty seasoned men. The *Susana* sailed from Boston Harbor, with Thomas Wake as her captain. Captain Wake was a former buccaneer pardoned by the 1688 Declaration of Amnesty, signed by King James II. Captain Wake decided to forgo his pardon and go on the account once again.

In January 1695 the four ships, commanded by Tew, left Newport for the Red Sea. By June of that year, Tew's fleet was stationed off Liparau Island at the mouth of the Red Sea. There he joined the pirate captains William May, commanding the *Pearl*, and Henry Every (a.k.a Henry Avery), commanding the *Fancy*. The squadron of pirate ships anchored there, waiting for any pilgrim fleet traveling south from Mocha, a port city in Yemen, on its way to Surat, India. Knowing the monsoon patterns of the region, the pirates realized any ships had to pass their waiting fleet.

Not sighting any Moorish ships for several weeks, an impatient Captain Every sent two of his men to Mocha on a reconnaissance mission. They returned with the news that a large combined merchant and pilgrim fleet of twenty-five richly loaded ships had left the port. If the ships continued at their current speed, they would be spotted on the horizon within a week. Setting their trap, the pirates sailed a short distance out to sea, waiting to pounce. A week later the fleet arrived. It being a moonless night, all the Indian merchantmen, filled with cargo, slipped past the pirate fleet unnoticed in the dead of night.

Enraged, Henry Every ordered all sails unfurled on the *Fancy*, ready for pursuit. However, a lookout on the *Fancy* noticed that two ships had fallen far behind the guarded Indian merchantmen. Captain Every turned his attention to those vessels. The *Amity* caught up with the *Fancy* and joined in the attack on the *Ganj-i-Sawai* (the *Gunsway*). The largest ship of the Moorish fleet with forty guns, it belonged to Grand Mogul Aurangzeb. The pilgrim ship was loaded with tribute and passengers. A three-hour battle to take the *Ganj-i-Sawai* raged.

During the attacks the *Dolphin* caught fire, requiring all hands to jump overboard, abandoning ship. Fortunately the men on the *Fancy* were able to rescue them from a watery grave. The *Portsmouth Adventure* and the *Susana*, both smaller ships, had fallen so behind the others, they never engaged in the actual fight.

The *Amity* suffered severe damage. Captain Tew was struck in the belly by a cannonball from the *Ganj-i-Sawai*. Charles Johnson gives a detailed account in his book: "In the Engagement, a Shot carry'd away the Rim of Tew's Belly, who held his Bowels with his Hands some small Space; when he dropp'd, it struck such a Terror in his Men, that they suffered themselves to be taken, without making Resistance."

Captain Johnson's version of events is not entirely true. Though the *Amity* was badly crippled and Tew died a horrid death, his shipmates helped capture the Indian merchantman. Crewmen on the *Amity* received a share of £1,000 ($500,000) for their participation in the fight. After several days of debauchery with their prisoners (that tale will be told in a later chapter), the men chose to return to St. Mary's. In December 1696 the *Amity* anchored off the island. The crew dispersed; some chose to stay on St. Mary's, while other continued to pursue pirating.

Colonel Benjamin Fletcher, for his brave service during the war in Ireland, became the royal governor of New York in 1692 by direct order of the new English King, William III. He was at a disadvantage from the very beginning of his commission, having been appointed to a position he was unequivocally unqualified for. Fletcher was an inexperienced statesman and diplomat. As a colonel he had been accustomed to having his every order fulfilled without question. He stepped into the governorship of a colony deeply in debt from the war.

He understood the strategic importance of defending English territory against constant raids from French troops billeted in Canada. He understood his orders did not just affect the politics of those who lived in New York province. He also needed to keep the English relationship with the powerful Iroquois Five Nations friendly. Up to that time the Iroquois aided the English militarily against the French raids into the various English colonies. Fletcher needed to make sure the Indian tribes did not become disillusioned with English assistance and choose to side with the French.

His orders, issued directly by the king, required him to build two major military forts in Albany and Schenectady (upstate New York). The forts were to strategically protect all the colonies (alternately referred to as provinces) from the French. However, the king's government in England had no intention of funding these projects or paying for their needed supplies. King William III ordered the monies to come from the New York colonial revenue or from direct financial contributions from its proud citizens. Furthermore, he commanded surrounding provinces to lend militia support to the forts when needed.

Since the forts in upper New York would also be protecting southern and central provinces, Governor Fletcher asked the other colonies for monetary assistance. The colonies steadfastly refused to provide money or militia. Because of the colonies' opposition,

King William III in 1693 granted Fletcher the title of commander-in-chief, with limited power over the militias of Connecticut. The king also appointed him governor of Pennsylvania. Each colony had individualized charters and resented the power that the king's direct orders afforded Fletcher. To them, the decree represented the end of their colonial individualism and the already limited power they had in the English government, and Parliament in particular.

Being the king's man, Fletcher called for a general assembly and tried to persuade Connecticut and Pennsylvania to cooperate peacefully. He did not succeed. Considering that men from New York were being called up to protect the other colonies from invasion, the heavily taxed populace of New York grew resentful of the continuing war and the other colonies. Disgruntled, many New Yorkers moved to unexplored territorial areas where there was no taxation. The New York colonial revenue began to decrease.

In response Governor Fletcher strictly enforced the Navigational Act that demanded taxation of every merchant ship that sailed into New York or up the Hudson River to the then free tax harbors of West and East Jersey.

To add to Benjamin Fletcher's problems, the Iroquois clan chiefs began to complain about the lack of militia support in the fight against the French. The Indians could not understand why the other English colonies didn't help the English New Yorkers. Fletcher discovered that the French commander had attempted on several occasions to sway the Indians to the French side. He worried the tribes might refuse to further assist the English altogether, or worse, fight alongside the French. He immediately sent his concerns to the Crown. In response King William III issued a decree that the colonies would lose their charters if they did not assist New York.

The colonies of West and East Jersey, along with Massachusetts, Maine, and Pennsylvania, begrudgingly complied. The combined colonies also came together, but in political opposition against Benjamin

Fletcher, his policies, and governmental decrees. They conspired to remove him from office any way they could. Colonial representatives from all the colonies bombarded the Board of Trade in England with any and all complaints concerning Fletcher's administration and the man himself. The colonial troubles then came down to a confrontation between the two political parties of Parliament, the Whigs and the Tories, to decide Fletcher's fate.

While New York revenue taxes continued to diminish, Fletcher increased the number of legally commissioned privateering letters of marque. Not only would the colony receive a monetary percentage from each commission, but Fletcher, along with his many appointed officials, did what other colonial officials were doing and took a personal percentage. While Governor Fletcher strictly adhered to the Navigational Acts for the legitimate merchant ships that sailed into New York Harbor, for a substantial bribe he and customs officials turned a blind eye to the pirate ships that anchored there. This charge, along with others concerning military embezzlement and bribed promotions, was brought to the Board of Trade with a demand for the governor's expulsion.

While visiting London, William Penn of Pennsylvania delivered a letter from New York assemblyman Peter Delanoy, an official in Fletcher's government, to the Board of Trade. The scathing letter contained a long list of accusations against Benjamin Fletcher. They ranged from him knowingly allowing fur traders to swindle Indians to embezzlement of military pay and supplies. The charge that received the most serious consideration was Delanoy's assertion that Fletcher was associating with pirates: "We have a parcel of pirates in these parts which [the people] call Red-Sea men, who often get great bootys of Arabian Gold. His Excellency gives all due encouragement to these men, because they make all due acknowledgements to him. . . . And now Sir that I have told you our distemper you will easily guesse at the cure we desire. It is the removal of this man, and we are not solicitous whether he is gently recalled or falls into disgrace, so we are rid of him."

From all the examples Delanoy listed, what concerned the Board of Trade most was specifically Fletcher's friendship with and aid to the Red Sea pirates. Within days of their receiving the damning letter from Delanoy, a disturbing communication came from the East India Company. The company described in detail the damage and havoc pirates caused in the Red Sea and Indian Ocean. Since the pirates all flew British colors during the attacks, the company feared a devastating reprisal against itself and its employees by the Grand Mogul and his people.

On June 22, 1696, Governor Fletcher sent a rebuttal of the accusations to the lords sitting on the Board of Trade. He professed his innocence of complicity in aiding pirates, especially those who sailed the Red Sea route: "Captain Tew brought no ship to this Port; he came here as a stranger and came to my table as other strangers do, when they come into the Province; he told me he had a sloop of force, well Manned and not only promised but entered into bond to make war upon the French in the mouth of Canada River, whereupon I gave him a commission and instructions according."

In the early months of 1697, all the compiled evidence against Fletcher was submitted to King William III. The king realized compromise was essential between the Crown and exclusively the colonies in North America concerning the grievances. On March 16, 1697, King William III ordered the Board of Trade to recall Fletcher from his position in North America.

His friend and patron Sir Robert Southwell came up with a plan to lessen the shame Fletcher would face on his arrival in England. Sir Southwell met with the king's secretary of state, Charles Talbot, Earl of Shrewsbury, with a consideration. Since Fletcher had not as yet received the news of his recall, perhaps it could be done "in such a manner as was proper for a gentleman who was not recalled for any fault committed, but because his Majesty thought it more for his service that his Government should be joined (harmoniously) to New England."

Talbot agreed to send Sir Southwell's request to the king. King William's reply was gracious. "His Majesty, having found no fault with Colonel Fletcher during his government, is pleased to allow of those favorable words, of taking care of him, and otherwise employing him, which are not unusual in letters of revocation."

On April 2, 1698, Governor Benjamin Fletcher was officially relieved of his post. The Board of Trade commissioned Richard Coote, the Earl of Bellomont, as his replacement. Though reams of proof concerning his corrupt dealings kept surfacing, Fletcher would return to England under favorable conditions.

The Earl of Bellomont refused to let Fletcher's corruption go without any repercussions. In his first act as governor, Bellomont would not permit Fletcher to board any ship back to England until Fletcher posted a bond of £10,000 ($5 million) to cover his alleged mismanagement of public funds. Driven, the Earl of Bellomont sent monthly correspondence to the Board of Trade concerning Fletcher's activities, believing the worst of these was Fletcher's overt association with pirates. Bellomont directly accused Fletcher of "encouragement of piracy, defrauding troops of their pay, and the willful neglect of the colony's defenses."

In his own defense Fletcher wrote a letter directly to the Board of Trade dated December 24, 1698. Among other personal conduct he defended, Fletcher specifically addressed his relationship with Thomas Tew.

As for my intimacy and kindness with Captain Tew and the great presents from him, which is objected, this is the truth and the whole truth of that poor affair. This Tew appeared to me not only a man of courage and activity, but of the greatest sense and remembrance of what he had seen, of any seaman I had met. He was also what they call a very pleasant man; so that at some times when the labors of my day were over it was some Divertisement as well as information to me to hear him talk. I wished in my mind to make him a sober man, and in particular to reclaim him from a vile habit of swearing. I gave him a boot to that purpose; and to gain more upon him, I gave him a gun of some value. In return thereof he made me also a present, which was a curiosity and in value not much; and this is the sum of all the kindness I am charged with; for as to the coming sometimes to my table, which I think was such as became my character, and hospitable to all, I hope that will not stick upon me, if your Lordships but inquire what others have done and still continue to do in that kind.

The Board of Trade hearings against Fletcher continued for years. The board did condemn him for encouraging piracy in New York province, and for not taking adequate security in regards to many suspicious men. They felt, however, his lack of vetting "suspected persons was not intentional."

The Earl of Bellomont, until his sudden death on March 5, 1701, pressed for further investigations into Fletcher's military embezzlement. But the muster rolls in question could not be located in the Military Pay Office. With lack of proof of any wrongdoing, and a change in the majority political party in Parliament, all accusations against Benjamin Fletcher were dropped. Colonel Fletcher returned to his home in Dublin, never to seek another public office. He died in 1703, his name and reputation ruined beyond repair.

CHAPTER SEVEN

Henry Every

BECAUSE OF HIS SUCCESSFUL EXPLOITS, HENRY EVERY BECAME THE most popular pirate in his own lifetime. As many pirates did, he was a man who answered to several names: Henry Avery, John Avery, Henry Every, Benjamin Bridgman, and "Long Ben," a nickname bestowed by his close friends. Regardless of which name was in fact his birthright, his successful attack on the Grand Mogul's pilgrim fleet in the Indian Ocean and the ramifications of that bold pirate attack fueled the imaginations of the English and North American populace. Henry Every and Thomas Tew became the forerunners of the successful Pirate Round.

As vague as the early lives of most pirates, it is suggested Henry Every was born on August 23, 1653, and raised in Plymouth, Devonshire, England. Though he was the son of a tavern keeper, like many in Plymouth he turned to the sea for a living. He joined the Royal Navy in 1689 under the name Henry Every. There are discrepancies as to which two naval ships he served on; they were either the HMS *Resolution* and HMS *Edgar*, or the HMS *Rupert* and HMS *Kent*. Having survived fierce sea battles early in the Nine Years' War (1688–1697), he was honorably discharged by 1690.

Seeking employment, Every signed on to a Royal African Company slave ship and sailed along the West African coast at the Bight of Benin. The ship made several trips to slave blocks along the eastern seaboard. Tired of the work, Every left after a few short years and returned to England in hopes of getting hired onto a merchantman.

Sir James Houblin, a member of the Parliament of the city of London and one of the founders of the Bank of England, was a merchant with a large fleet of ships. Since England and Spain were allies against the French, Sir Houblin leased two of his ships, the *Duke* and the *Duchess*, to the command of Don Arthuro Bourne, who represented the Spanish interest. While waiting for the ships' names to be legally changed and painted on their sterns to read the *Charles* (in honor of Spain's king) and the *James* (his brother), respectively, Every secured the post as first mate on the *Charles*, under Captain Charles Gibson. Don Arthuro Bourne commanded the *James* with Captain Humphrey.

The two ships sailed to the city of Corunna on the northwest coast of Spain, there to await cargo, passengers, and more important their letter of marque. Don Bourne informed Henry Every that their commission was not only to sail cargo and passengers to various cities along the Spanish Main, but also to become "guarda del costa." They were to prevent Frenchmen sailing out of the harbors of Martinique and Guadeloupe islands from smuggling goods into the various ports along the Spanish Main. The Spanish government hated the fact its revenue stream on taxed expensive goods and food was diminished because the French provided cheaper products.

After the ships landed at Corunna, the crews aboard the *Charles* and *James* did not receive their promised wages for sailing across the water. Corunna, or "the Groin," as the English seamen called that area, is a bastardized version of the Spanish word *groyne*, which describes a breakwater jetty that separates the sea from the bay at a peninsula like Corunna.

To make matters worse, the crews spent the next eight months aboard their vessels waiting for the promised cargo, passengers, and coveted letter of marque that never came. Understanding they were on the privateer wage of "no prey, no pay," the men grew increasingly restless and mad. It did not help their temperament to watch Captain Gibson's nightly drinking bouts below deck or his many trips ashore, while they were being increasingly confined to their ships.

Joseph Dann of Rochester, one of Every's crewmates, later recounted the decision that began Captain Every's fame: "The Shipps Company mutinied at Corunna for want of their pay, there being 8 months due to them; some of the men proposed to Captain Every, who was master [the navigator] of the *Charles*, to carry away the Shipp, which was agreed on sworne too; accordingly they sayld from Corunna the 7th of May 1694."

Having accepted his shipmate's votes, Henry Every woke Captain Charles Gibson from a drunken slumber and offered him the opportunity to join with the crew and sail to the Red Sea. Captain Gibson, with fifteen others, refused to join the mutineers. Guaranteeing they would come to no harm, Every had the men rowed ashore. The mutineers, however, forced the ship's surgeon to remain aboard the *Charles*. Between seventy and eighty men stayed with Captain Every.

When seamen aboard the *James* saw the longboat being lowered into the sea, they called to the *Charles* for answers. When the men signaled back of their mutiny, twenty-five men from the *James*, already knowing of the mutinous plans and intending on joining in the pirate adventure, had already lowered a longboat into the water and were rowing toward the *Charles*.

Hearing the shouting, Captain Humphrey aboard the *James* rushed on deck and ordered his crew to fire onto the longboat and the deserters. All the shots splashed into the sea. Desperate, Captain Humphrey called out to a Dutch ship, the *Mynheer*, anchored in the harbor. Humphrey offered a grand reward if she would raise her anchor and head off the *Charles*. The captain of the *Mynheer* graciously refused to take sides. Every navigated the *Charles* safely out of the Spanish harbor. His quartermaster, having taken stock of the provisions aboard, discovered fifteen tons of food along with an ample supply of ammunition for the forty guns on the main deck and rifles.

When the loyal crew from the *Charles* finally reached London, one of the seamen allegedly carried a ballad written by Captain Every to the publisher Theophilius Lewis, entitled "A Copy of Verses, Composed by Captain Henry Every, Lately Gone to Sea to seek his Fortune." The first verse inspired men to piracy, and with the ballad's publication Henry Every became a folk hero.

> Come all you brave boys, whose courage is bold,
> Will you venture with me? I'll gut you with gold.
> Make waste unto Coruna: a ship you will find.
> That's called the Fancy, will pleasure your mind.
> Captain Every is in her, and calls her his own;
> He will box her about, boys, before he has done.
> French, Spaniard, and Portuguese, the heathen likewise,
> He has made a war with them until that he dies.

Renaming the ship the *Fancy,* they sailed south along the coast of Africa. Captain Every took every opportunity to pick up more provisions for the long voyage to the Red Sea. He also knew more men would be needed when, not if, they ran into a tough cannon battle. But he didn't have to worry on that score; men hearing of the intended voyage eagerly signed up to crew aboard her.

Their luck began as the *Fancy* sailed by the Cape Verde Islands. At the first stop, Boa Vista, they purchased salt, a valuable commodity for drying meats, and then they continued to sail to the Isle of Maio (Isle of May). Before entering the harbor the pirates spotted three English ships anchored in the calm waters. Every sailed into the harbor with English colors flying high on the mainmast of the *Fancy.* Catching them off guard, the pirates ransacked the three ships for food, provisions, an anchor, and some cable and encouraged nine more men to sign the *Fancy*'s articles of agreement.

Sailing along the coast of Guinea, the pirates stole a quantity of gold dust from a group of natives intending on trading for provisions.

Once the natives boarded the *Fancy*, the pirates jumped them, forcing the natives into shackles and taking them below deck. They remained aboard with the pirates' full intention of selling the men at the first opportunity. After measuring the precious gold dust, the quartermaster concluded they had confiscated five pounds of it.

Needing to careen their ship, the *Fancy* headed for the Bight of Biafra. While there the crew voted to sail next to the "Prince's Island" of Principe, St. Thomé, and Annobon in Equatorial Guinea to see what fortunes lay there for them. For a safe anchorage, Captain Every presented the Portuguese official a gift of seven of the shackled natives.

The pirates didn't consider other ships in the harbor off-limits. The crew of the *Fancy* boarded two Danish vessels. After a hand-to-hand skirmish, the pirates captured the ships. Joseph Dann later recounted that they took flintlocks, chests of linen, and perpetuanna (a durable woolen fabric), along with a great quantity of brandy and approximately forty pounds of gold dust. After ransacking the two ships, Captain Every offered to return the smaller Dutch ship to its commander. Her captain, also being the ship owner's representative, refused, stating the owner had insured the ship and after all the fighting it was worthless in its present condition. The pirates put the Dutch crews ashore, burnt the smaller ship, and kept the larger of the two. Nine Dutchmen eagerly signed on under Captain Every.

Hopping from one island to the next, always on the search for provisions, the new pirate fleet sailed to the safety of Fernando Po Island, west of Guinea, and careened both ships. At Cape Lopez, on the tip of Gabon, Africa, they purchased honey from a small merchantman. Disliking how the captain treated his crew, Every's men promptly burnt the man's vessel. They traded food with a Portuguese slaver for clothing, along with bolts of trade silks. While barrels of water and armaments were being loaded, Captain Every purchased dozens of cattle to have slaughtered and salted for the long trip ahead. Purchasing their final provisions on Annobon Island, off Equatorial Guinea, they were set for the long voyage. Excitement over the "adventure," as they called their journey, meant more men from the island joined the *Fancy's* growing numbers. The pirates sailed around the Cape of Good Hope and on to Madagascar without incident.

Again underway, it quickly became apparent to those aboard that many of Captain Every's men had contracted one of the numerous unknown fevers plaguing Europeans in Africa. Since Captain Every had already intended to stop at the island of Johanna before heading to the Red Sea, he dropped his sick mates off on the island. Johanna is an island in the Comoro island chain between northern Madagascar and mainland Africa.

Before he could resupply the *Fancy*, three English East India ships appeared at the mouth of the harbor. Not wanting to be trapped, Every ordered the ships to sea, barely outrunning the East Indiamen. The *Fancy* made it safely to the island of Patta, near Kenya, where it remained anchored for weeks.

Finally returning to Johanna to retrieve their shipmates who survived the fever, Every heard encouraging news. A ruling on January 11, 1694, by the House of Commons had dismantled the monopoly of the British East India Company concerning exclusive trade rights with India and other countries along the Indian Ocean. Now knowing any English subject could legally trade with India, the crew of the *Fancy* was eager to set sail. Before the ship left Johanna, Captain Every handed a letter to one of the native chieftains, asking him to deliver the missive, after their departure, to the first English ship that sailed into port. It simply stated the pirates' intentions, and how an English ship was safe from their guns if, upon sighting the *Fancy*, it flew its flags in an unusual formation:

To all English Commanders, lett this Satisfye, that I was Riding here att this Instant in ye Ship Fancy Man of Warr, formerly the Charles of ye Spanish Expedition, who departed from Croniae [Corunna] ye 7th of May 1694. Being (and am now) in a Ship of

46 Guns 150 Men and bound to Seek our Fortunes. I have never as Yett Wronged any English or Dutch, nor ever Intend whilst I am Commander. Wherefore as I commonly speak with all Ships, I Desire whoever Comes to ye perusal of this to take this Signall, That if you, or aney whome you may informe, are desirous, to know what wee are att a Distance, Then make your Antient Vp [ensign flag] up in a Ball or Bundle and hoyst him att ye Mizon Pekk ye Mizon Being furled I shall answer with same & Never Molest you: for my Men are hungry Stout and Resolute: should they Exceed my Desire I cannot help my selfe.

> *As yett*
> *An Englishman's Friend*
> *Att Johanna February ye 28th, 1695/4*
> *Henry Every*

Conveniently, Every seemed to have forgotten about the English and Dutch ships they had plundered on their way to Madagascar. Though legal trade was not uppermost in his mind, perhaps he felt by issuing his letter, from that point on none of his men would be punished if they stole only from "heathen Moors." Captain Every, perhaps in an attempt to further ingratiate himself and his crew to the authorities, added a postscript of warning: "Here is 160 french armed men now att Mohilla [a state in Africa] who waits for opportunity of getting aney ship, take Care of you selves."

One of the same English East India ships that had earlier attempted to capture the *Fancy* received the missive. Captained by Leonard Edgcumbe, the East Indiaman sailed directly to Mohilla. They found the Frenchmen ashore with a damaged ship. The English seamen plundered the vessel, burnt her, and took six of the Frenchmen prisoners to Bombay, India. In May 1695 they handed the French prisoners and Henry Every's letter to Sir John Gayer, governor at Bombay, with a full report of their encounters at Johanna. Every's notice caused mixed reaction among the Englishmen living in India.

Some viewed him as a patriot and privateer sailing against their enemies. Others considered him and his crew pirates who needed to be captured by any and all means.

By then the *Fancy*'s pirate crew had finally set sail for their intended destination. In August they anchored off Perim Island, at

Captain Henry Every, with the *Fancy* shown engaging its prey in the background.
CREDIT: UNKNOWN, C. 1712

the narrowest point on the Strait of Bab el Mandeb, the southern-most end of the Red Sea. To their surprise, they encountered Captain Thomas Tew's ship, the *Amity*, and his fleet of the *Dolphin*, *Portsmouth Adventure*, *Pearl*, and *Susana*. The men on Tew's five vessels had heard of Henry Every's plans while their ships were all being outfitted on St. Mary's Island. To a man, the pirates believed Captain Every the most experienced and agreed to join his plan for the ensuing battle and sharing in the overall prizes.

After waiting at Perim Island for five weeks, Captain Every dispatched crewmates to Mocha. They reported back that a combined merchant and pilgrim fleet of twenty-five ships was heading in their direction, making for the homeport of Surat, India. The Indian fleet, being forewarned of the trap by a passing merchant ship, sailed past undetected during a moonless night. The *Fancy's* lookout spotted a lone straggler. For five days Every sailed the *Fancy* in pursuit, not caring if the other ships in his fleet could keep up. On approach to Cape Guardafui (Gees Gardafuul), Somalia, he trapped the unarmed merchant ship *Fateh Mohammed*, which was owned by the most influential and richest Indian trader of the day, Abd-ul Ghafur. Carrying gold and silver worth £50,000 to £60,000 ($25 million to $30 million). The Indian crew offered no resistance and surrendered.

Ordering a few pirates to remain aboard the *Fateh Mohammed* and guard their prize, Captain Every turned his attention to the pilgrim ship, which was desperately tacking to outsail the *Fancy* to Surat and safety. The Grand Mogul's ship *Ganj-i-Sawai* (anglicized to *Gunsway*), meaning "Exceeding Treasure," was returning from a pilgrimage to Mecca. The six hundred passengers aboard were diplomats, along with their families and concubines, as well as a daughter and aunt of the Grand Mogul. Both ladies sailed with their entire retinues of servants and slaves. Captained by Ibrahim Khan, the *Ganj-i-Sawai* had sixty-two guns mounted on her deck, four hundred armed soldiers, plus a sailing crew of one hundred.

The *Fancy* attacked the pilgrim ship with a vengeance. Captain Tew on the *Amity* came alongside and joined in the battle. Unaccustomed to fighting and terrified of the voracity of the attack, Captain Khan ran below deck and hid in a locked cabin. Khafi Khan, an Indian historian that lived during that time, recorded that survivors had testified Captain Khan also armed a dozen of the slave girls with guns and ordered them on deck to fight beside the soldiers.

Indian soldiers were never trained to take the initiative during a skirmish. Without the ship's captain to issue orders, the soldiers floundered as the pirates fired round after round of cannonballs toward the ship. The sailors on the *Ganj-i-Sawai* managed to return some fire, but in the panic that ensued, the pirates boarded the ship with little resistance.

The pirate fleet towed the two captured ships to the calm waters of nearby Socotra Island. For days they anchored alongside the disabled Indian ships, wreaking havoc in their frenzied debauchery. With the exception of the Grand Mogul's daughter, every woman aboard, young or old, was raped multiple times, some dying from the abuse. Men were brutally tortured and killed. The accounts state many men and women committed suicide before they could be attacked. Those who died from the pirates' cruel handling were unceremoniously dumped overboard.

Once satiated, and with the ships plundered of anything of value, the pirates let those who survived continue on their journey. Badly damaged with the mainmast shot off and her sails punctured with cannon shot, the *Ganj-i-Sawai* drifted back to the port of Surat. News traveled through the country. The outrage over the attack inflamed the population to violence against the East India Company and its employees. The government of England had to act and act quickly.

The pirates had no concern for the political and economic ramifications of their attack on the *Ganj-i-Sawai*. Once safely back in Madagascar, the pirates inventoried and divided their plunder. The two Indian vessels yielded over half a million gold and silver coins, gold bars, one hundred thousand solid gold sequins, chests of silk, chests of various loose gems and diamonds, and a gold-trimmed saddle and bridle encrusted with rubies that was to be presented to the Grand Mogul. The estimated worth of the entire cargo came to approximately £600,000 ($300 million).

Each pirate over 18 years old received £1,000 ($500,000) and a purse of cut and uncut gems as his share. Those under the age of 18 received £500 ($250,000) and a purse of gems. The share of the few boys under the age of 14 was £100 ($50,000) so they could "apprentice themselves to an honest trade ashore."

Before returning to the North American colonies, Henry Every planned to stop first in the Bahamas. He wanted to assess the political climate once news of their attack became widely known. But the majority of the pirates refused to sail to an English-held island. Being outvoted, in November 1695 Captain Every sailed the men who didn't wish to remain on Madagascar to the French colony on Bourbon Island (renamed Réunion Island), situated east of Madagascar. Once anchored off Bourbon Island, over half of the remaining crew on the *Fancy* departed with their plunder.

In April 1696 Captain Every, with a crew of 115 men, anchored the *Fancy* off the island of New Providence as planned. For the safe harbor, the pirates generously offered the proprietary governor of the island, Sir Nicholas Trott, twenty pieces of eight from the ship's shared booty, plus two gold coins from each crewman. Henry Every personally offered to double his share. Knowing the *Fancy* would soon be too recognizable to sail to the colonies, Captain Every posed as an unsuccessful privateer who needed to sell the ship. After each pirate received his share, many purchased their own ships or passages to England, Ireland, or other friendly islands.

With Every's share of the *Fancy*'s sale he purchased a sloop, crewed by those pirates who desired to return to the colonies. Not wishing to be discovered, Every quietly dropped off small parties of his men up and down the New England coast, men who were willing to take their chances on land. His destination was Boston Harbor.

By the time Captain Every set foot in Boston, news of the enormity of the Grand Mogul attack had reached not only England, but North America as well. The wealth reported in the broadsheets and newspapers not only astonished the public, but also made Henry Every's name a popular household word.

Writers of romantic chapbooks, the first inexpensive books the general public could afford, seized on the story of Every. The stories of pirates, along with fascination for the exotic Indian culture and suggested sexual innuendo, fired the public's imagination. Numerous ballads and stories turned Captain Every into a gentleman pirate and the love interest of the Grand Mogul's daughter, or granddaughter, depending on the chapbook. In 1709 a book was published by the fictional Dutch author Captain Van Broeck: *The Life and Adventures of Captain John Avery, now in Possession of Madagascar.* In the book Captain Every not only marries the Indian princess, but also creates a vast fortress kingdom on St. Mary's Island, occupied by thousands of loyal pirates and natives.

In 1713 a play by Charles Johnson entitled *The Successful Pyrate,* based on the life and adventures of Henry Every, premiered at the Theatre Royal in Drury Lane, London. The production ran for years and also had a successful run in the colonies. The author Daniel Defoe, of *Robinson Crusoe* fame, wrote *The King of Pirates* in 1719, supposedly based on interviews between Henry Every and himself.

The political and economic fallout from the raid on the *Ganj-i-Sawai* was enormous. Upon hearing the news concerning the capture of the pilgrim ship and the inhuman treatment of the passengers, the people of Surat formed an angry mob and stormed the headquarters of the East India Company. They stoned one employee to death before the local Indian governor, Itimad Khan, was able to save the other Englishmen. He arrested the remaining forty English employees and, while he waited for the Grand Mogul to decide their fate, had them chained in a windowless prison for over a year.

Able to pass letters back and forth through loyal Indian employees, the Englishmen sent a letter requesting help to Sir John Gayer, a company man and also the governor of Bombay. Sir Gayer immediately notified the Board of Trade in London of the situation. He impressed upon the board the urgency of somehow lessening the situation in India. He stated that the Grand Mogul had not only ordered an attack on every Englishman in Bombay, but in his rage, the closing down of all English trade to the country.

Samuel Annesley, an East India Company representative, promised the Grand Mogul compensation, with a note of credit from the Bank of England, for his financial losses. He also guaranteed that from that moment on, large, armed East India Company vessels would accompany all pilgrim ships to and from Mecca.

In addition, Annesley swore that the English government, along with the full support of the East India Company, would actively spare no effort in capturing Henry Every, his crew, and any other pirate cruising in his territory. The Grand Mogul accepted Mr. Annesley's terms and called off the attack on Bombay. Yet he refused any trade to commence between England and India, or the release of the English prisoners, until Henry Every was hanged in chains.

Annesley saw the promise of the company ships accompanying pilgrim fleets as a wonderful opportunity for the company. It would help their status as well as create an independent political entity with great influential powers over the creation of governmental laws. By May 1696 Sir Gayer wrote to the Board of Trade, informing it that the East India Company had searched for Captain Every with no success. Sir Gayer had to conclude that Henry Every most likely had sailed to the New England area, where he would be welcomed. That being the case, he felt that the pirates had sailed away from the company's jurisdiction and were now England's problem to solve.

On August 10, 1696, the Board of Trade drafted a decree for King William III to sign. The proclamation was addressed to every colonial governor suspected of harboring pirates. It left little room for interpretation: "Whereas we formerly received information from the Governor and Company of Merchants in London Trading with the West Indies that one Henry Every . . . had under English colours committed several acts of piracy upon the seas of Persia . . . We do hereby command all His Majesty's Governor Commanders . . . to seize and apprehend the said Henry Every."

The colonial governors' responses were to the point. They had no knowledge of the whereabouts of Captain Every or any of his crew.

To hasten the reopening of trade with India, East India Company officials posted a £50 ($25,000) reward for each of Every's crewmates and a £100 ($50,000) reward for Henry Every's capture, later to be raised to £500 ($250,000).

Some of Every's crewmates were not too fortunate. Joseph Dawson, Edward Forseith, William May, William Bishop, James Lewis, and John Sparkes sailed a ship into Westport, County Mayo, Ireland, on the June 7, 1696. They brought attention to themselves by unloading chests of gold and silver Arabian coin, along with silks and other exotic items.

John Dann and Philip Middleton were eventually captured. They both willingly turned king's witness against the others. Dann revealed in his court statement the details of their numerous piratical activities, and the senseless brutality of their attacks on the passengers of the *Ganj-i-Sawai*.

The prosecution attempted to impress upon the jury the necessity of finding the men guilty. His main argument against the pirates hinged on the fact that all commerce with India had stopped. Without a guilty conviction for piracy, commerce would never resume. Not only that, but the Grand Mogul of India would declare war against the Englishmen now living in Bombay and the English Empire as a whole. The prosecutor's main argument against the alleged pirates was their attack on a heathen Moorish ship and a private company's profit losses. The men sitting on the jury did not consider actions against a heathen ship as being piratical. Nor did it concern them one bit that the East India Company was losing daily profits. What a great surprise for the Crown's prosecutor on October 19, 1696, when the jury returned a verdict of not guilty. Needing to be able to prove to their allies, and the Grand Mogul, that the government was actively pursuing and executing pirates, the court ordered the men be returned to prison to await another trial.

Stacking the jury with individuals more sympathetic to the government's case, the prosecution retried the six men on charges of piracy against English shipping. This time the pirates were found guilty, and on November 25, 1696, all six were hanged at Execution Dock in London.

By his actions Henry Every inadvertently brought the tiny island of St. Mary's into notice. The recognition became the death knell for the island. Under severe government scrutiny, few pirates or deserting sailors dared to settle or trade on the island. By 1699 New York merchants no longer chose the island as a trade destination.

Once he dropped off his last crewmate in Boston, what of the man himself? There are stories of Henry Every living in Ireland and being scammed by merchants, living in Edinburgh, falling into extreme poverty, living in the colonies, or returning to St. Mary's under the name Benjamin Bridgman. His notoriety continued for years. But Every was never captured or officially heard from again.

Chapter Eight

William Kidd

It is easy to assume that whatever the end of Henry Every's life was, he had little concern for the ramifications of his attack on the Grand Mogul's ship. Ironically, because of that attack, another man, who never intended to become a pirate, would go down in history as one of the most notorious of them all . . . one William Kidd.

The son of Reverend John Kidd, William was born in 1645, in the town of Greenock twenty-five miles west of Glasgow, Scotland. It is unclear at what age he first went to sea. He was a powerfully built man who stood taller than the average height of five-foot-five to five-foot-six for men of that era. He was known for his violent, uncontrollable temper and bullying. When drunk it was not unusual for him to physically threaten anyone who disagreed with his opinion. Along the docks William Kidd was a braggart, continually commenting on his own importance because of his political and social connections, not to mention his success as a sailor during King William's War. His reputation as a successful seaman was widely known among merchants and plantation owners, but he was not respected by any of the men who sailed under his various commands.

By August of 1689 Kidd became the captain of the privateer *Blessed William* (no relation), sailing the West Indies. Kidd decided to assist the Royal Navy squadron under the command of Captain

Hewetson on the HMS *Lion* in raiding the French-held island of Marie Galante (south of Guadeloupe and North of Dominica). Praised for his actions, he continued to assist Captain Hewetson during a deadly battle against five French warships off the island of St. Martin. The English being triumphant, Captain Kidd sailed the *Blessed William* to the island of Nevis for refitting the battle damage and restocking provisions and ammunition.

But Kidd's crewmates had signed up for privateering, not being under the strict command of the Royal Navy. While Kidd was ashore they voted to mutiny and sailed away, taking the *Blessed William* and Kidd's prize money of £2,000 ($1 million).

Stranded and furious at his crew's betrayal, Kidd fortunately received a captured French ship from the governor of Nevis as a thank you for his protection against the French raiders. With his new vessel *Antegoa* (*Antigua*), Kidd hastily gathered a crew and set sail to apprehend the *Blessed William* and exact his revenge. Kidd followed the mutineers to New York, where he was shocked to discover they had sold the *Blessed William* and signed on to the *Jacob*, sailing to the Indian Ocean and out of his reach.

Kidd reached New York at the most advantageous time for his political and social career. It was an important political city, and civil war had just broken out there. When it became known that Prince William had taken the throne of England, Jacob Leisler, a loyal subject of King James II, seized power in the city. King William III, to cement his authority in the province of New York, appointed Colonel Henry Sloughter as the new governor. Sloughter's orders included executing Leisler for heresy. In January 1691 Sloughter's troops arrived in New York without incident. Unfortunately, Colonel Sloughter's ship had run aground at Bermuda.

In the interim, troop commander Colonel Richard Ingoldesby requested Leisler's surrender. Leisler's answer was to rally those loyal to King James II and take over Fort James, situated at the tip of Manhattan. A fierce battle ensued with many dead and wounded, but no clear victor. Captain Kidd, who supported King William III, loaded the *Antegoa* with guns and needed ammunition and reached Colonel Ingoldesby's base camp in time to prepare the fort for another assault.

Governor Sloughter's ship arrived mid-March. Kidd sailed out with King William loyalists to warn Sloughter of the situation. Governor Sloughter's troops were able to quell the revolt and execute Leisler for treason. The city of New York became split into two vicious rival political factions.

For Kidd's assistance in squelching the uprising, Governor Sloughter awarded Kidd £150 ($75,000). Because of his actions against Leisler, Captain Kidd acquired a very powerful and influential circle of friends. He decided to remain in New York and woo the very wealthy and attractive trice-widowed Sarah Bradley Oort. Kidd married Sarah on May 16, 1691, mere days after the death of her husband, John Oort. By virtue of his marriage, Kidd inherited substantial amounts of property in and around Manhattan.

The Kidd family moved into a fine mansion located along the East River at 119-121 Pearl Street, just north of the city's business district. William continued to sail as a privateer against the French, which enabled him to purchase his own fleet of ships from his prize money. In addition, the family purchased a pew at the influential Anglican Trinity Church, counting many local politicians as friends.

In 1693 one of his acquaintances, Robert Livingston, purchased a tract of property from Kidd to build a private ship dock. One year later, while serving as the foreman of a grand jury, Kidd refused to indict Livingston on charges of knowingly trading with the enemy during war.

Back in London, Richard Coote, the First Earl of Bellomont, had powerful political friends who knew Bellomont to be financially in the red. They managed to get Bellomont appointed as the new governor of Massachusetts. Though the governorship was a political position of power, believing the position should be held by a Massachusetts-born man the Massachusetts colonists did not consistently pay their royal

A romanticized depiction of Captain William Kidd greeting guests in New York Harbor.
CREDIT: JEAN LEON GEROME FERRIS, C. 1932

governors. Since New York had established a consistent, impressive salary for its governor, his friends around Parliament strongly hinted that Bellomont should also be handed the position of New York governor.

However, Benjamin Fletcher was the governor of New York at the time. Bellomont's allies began a campaign to besmirch Fletcher to the Board of Trade, get him removed, and move Bellomont into the governorship. The plan succeeded with the help of Robert Livingston. Livingston served as commissary, the person responsible for supplying food to the English troops at Fort Albany and New York. At times Livingston used his own funds to feed the troops, and he had demanded that Fletcher pay back the money. Believing Livingston a wealthy enough man to wait until after the war to get reimbursed, Fletcher refused. Furious, Livingston sailed to London and colluded with the Earl of Bellomont and his allies to get Benjamin Fletcher removed and the Earl of Bellomont sworn into office.

In the early months of 1695, William Kidd was summoned to London as a witness against Governor Fletcher at the Board of Trade fraud hearing. Additionally, he hoped to procure privateering and trade letters of marque. He came into the social circle of the Earl of Bellomont, who first appeared to be Kidd's friend, only to later become his nemesis.

Livingston had also traveled to England to testify against Fletcher, and while there he met socially with Kidd. Livingston, traveling in higher social circles than Kidd, had attempted to interest Bellomont and his cronies since August 1695 in forming a shipping syndicate. He proposed they invest in outfitting a ship, sail against the French and pirates, and divvy up the profits. With Kidd now in London, Livingston suggested him as the most qualified captain for the expedition. With the French still at war with England and piracy on the rise, the men begrudgingly agreed to the venture. When approached with the proposition, and without knowing all of the details, Kidd eagerly jumped at the opportunity.

Unbeknownst to Kidd, the syndicate comprised esteemed men of political power. Along with Livingston and Kidd, the investors included Charles Montague, the First Earl of Halifax, Chancellor of the Exchequer; Lord Somers, the Lord Chancellor and Keeper of the Great Seal of England; Charles Talbot, the First Duke of Shrewsbury, and Henry Sydney, the Earl of Romney, two Secretaries of State; Edward Russell, the First Earl of Oxford, the First Lord High Admiral of the fleet and treasurer of the Navy; Sir Edward Harrison, director of the East India Company and a wealthy city merchant; Richard Coote, the Earl of Bellomont; Samuel Bradley; as well as King William III himself.

With the exception of the king, each man contributed to the purchase of a thirty-four-gun ship, the *Adventure Galley*, and her supplies. The ship was a hybrid design and unusual for its time. It not only maneuvered under sail, but came outfitted with forty-six oars, twenty-three to a side. If the sails or winds failed, the *Adventure Galley* could be rowed a brisk three miles per hour.

The documents stated that the Earl of Bellomont, the figurehead of the syndicate, would receive 60 percent of all profits and redistribute the wealth to the silent investors. Kidd and his crew would divide up the rest. Lord Shrewsbury arranged with Bellomont to assign a 10 percent share to the king. With King William's approval of the venture, any prizes Kidd captured would bypass the declaration of cargo that customarily required all cargos be reported to the admiralty courts for taxation.

King William III signed the first commission, called a Commission of Reprisals, which had been written by the Earl of Bellomont. Signed on December 11, 1695, the letter of marque authorized Kidd to "set forth in warlike manner, the ship called the *Adventure Galley*, under his own command, and therewith by force of arms to apprehend, seize, and take the ships, vessels, and goods belonging to the French King and his subjects . . . and such other ships, vessels and goods as are or shall be liable to confiscation."

Either Kidd did not read all the conditions written in this first commission, or he chose to ignore them. It required him to keep a journal of all his captured prizes with a detailed account of their capture. In addition, it held Kidd personally liable for any breach of commission protocol in sailing a prize ship into port and having it officially condemned before selling its contents and the vessel.

Realizing the terms he had agreed to, Kidd, contrary to many accounts, did not eagerly agree to take the commissions. Guessing who the syndicate silent partners were, he tried to back out of the deal. During Kidd's trial for murder and piracy, his old commander Colonel Hewetson, testifying in his defense, stated that Kidd had confided to him "that he did not want to go into the enterprise at all, but said [to Hewetson] that Lord Bellomont told him there were great men and they would stop his brigantine, the *Antegoa* in the river [Thames], if he did not accede."

It also stated that the ship's crew were knowingly sailing under a "no purchase (prize), no pay" contract. In addition, if prize money and goods valued at £100,000 ($50 million) or more were delivered to Bellomont in Boston, the *Adventure Galley* would become the personal property of Kidd. The caveat to this first letter of marque stated if the venture proved unsuccessful, Kidd had to repay Bellomont the entire amount the syndicate invested by March 25, 1697. It also required Kidd to post a bond of £20,000 ($10 million) to ensure that Bellomont would receive his personal initial investment if Kidd were unsuccessful.

King William III issued Kidd his second letter of marque commission to seize pirates on January 26, 1696.

> . . . *under your Command, full Power and Authority to apprehend, seize, and take into your Custody as well the said Captain Thomas Too [Thomas Tew of Rhode Island], John Ireland, Captain Thomas Wake and Captain William Maze, or Mace [of New York], as all such Pyrates, Free Booters and Sea Rovers, being either our Subjects, or of other Nations . . . which you shall meet with upon the Seas; or Coasts of America, or upon any other Seas or Coasts.*

Edward Harrison of the East India Company insisted on selecting the ship's crew. Afraid they would too easily turn to piracy once out of English waters, Harrison refused to sign on the account any Scot or American colonist who applied.

On April 23, 1696, Captain Kidd sailed out of Plymouth, England, with a crew of approximately eighty men. Since the war still raged, only half of Kidd's crew had any sailing experience. Captain Kidd's arrogance played against him once more. It was the custom of ships sailing from an English port to acknowledge any naval ship they passed with a gun salute. Having the king personally sign his letters of marque, Kidd felt the *Adventure Galley* was an equal to any naval ship, and by that logic he a commissioned naval officer.

Therefore, he did not lower his flag or fire a salute in acknowledgement of the Royal Navy ships as they sailed out of the harbor. One of the naval ships fired a shot across the *Adventure Galley*'s bow as a reminder of this courtesy. Not only did Kidd refuse again to fire a gun salute or lower his flag, but the men on the topsails of Kidd's vessel actually dropped their pants and mooned the naval ships as the *Adventure Galley* sailed past.

Enraged by the insult, word quickly passed throughout the fleet. Barely had the *Adventure Galley* sailed onto open waters when the HMS *Duchess* hailed her. Under the Defense of the Realm Act, the navy during wartime could impress men from any ship while it was at sea. The *Duchess* press-ganged the majority of Kidd's crew, leaving him barely enough men to handle the ship. Kidd was forced to return to England and through official channels petitioned for the return of his men. Because the king was a silent partner in Kidd's venture, the HMS *Duchess* received orders to return the men taken off the *Adventure Galley*. Under protest the naval ship returned the exact number of men, but not the same men, handing Kidd a motlier crew.

Instead of sailing straight to Madagascar, Kidd had no choice but to sail first to New York and sign on more men for the voyage. On the way they captured a French ship, the *Sita Gratia*, and brought her into New York Harbor. Kidd's privateering commissions stated any captured ship was to be condemned and sold for profit, and 10 percent of the sale was to be handed to the governor. However, the Earl of Bellomont was not yet officially the governor of New York at the time of the sale; Benjamin Fletcher still held the post. The Earl of Bellomont was furious when news reached him that Kidd had handed Fletcher the prize money Bellomont felt he should have received.

Word spread throughout New York and New England that Kidd was signing men up for a privateering journey. To encourage men to join the adventure, Kidd wrote out a set of ship's articles that to many, once in the hands of the authorities, appeared suspiciously similar to the articles pirates signed before they sailed. Kidd was so convinced he would encounter enemy ships for prize money, he promised the men they would be paid for their work. Kidd did not specify to the men the "no prey, no pay" conditions of his commission until the ship was far out to sea. It immediately created a great degree of desperation in his crew to find as many enemy ships as they could to capture.

Men, some of very dubious character and reputation, flocked to sign on the account. Realizing the majority of men who joined had little or no experience with blue water sailing or sea battles, Captain Kidd hoped the long months of sailing would afford the men ample time to hone their skills before any enemy confrontations.

On September 6, 1696, with a compliment of 152 crewmen aboard, the *Adventure Galley* set sail. By the time William Kidd sailed out of New York, the news of Henry Every's attack was well known throughout England and the American colonies.

It was not until January 27, 1697, that the *Adventure Galley* dropped anchor at the port of Tulear (Toliara) on the west coast of Madagascar. With many of the crew sick with scurvy, they remained there until late February. Desperately needing to careen the ship of Teredo worms and barnacles that attach themselves to a ship's hull bottom, destroying the wood, Kidd sailed his ship to the sandy island of Mohilla. In the three months it took to make the ship seaworthy, Kidd lost another thirty men to disease.

Now safe to sail, Kidd set course to Johanna in the Comoro Islands (off the southeast coast of Africa). The island, with its abundance of fresh fruits and vegetables, had become a popular stop for English ships heading for India. With the natives friendly to Europeans, captains and crews enjoyed the island life while they waited for the April southwesterly monsoon winds that made the voyage north accessible. While waiting, the *Adventure Galley* lost another twenty men to plague.

Kidd found himself in a tight spot in April of 1697. According to the contract he had signed with the Earl of Bellomont, he had already missed the March deadline to pay him back or face financial ruin. Kidd needed to find a prize not only for himself, but also for his crewmen, who were feeling desperate. He could have tried to catch known pirates heading to St. Mary's Island with their rich prizes. However, Kidd knew his inexperienced crew didn't have a chance against seasoned pirates. He had not heard of any French ships within the area. In the hopes of encountering a treasure-laden pilgrim fleet, Kidd made the decision to sail to the Red Sea.

Arriving at Perim Island, a favorite spot for pirate attacks, Kidd sent spies to Mocha for reconnaissance. He was not disappointed when they returned with news of a fifteen-ship fleet heading their way. Excited, the men of the *Adventure Galley* prepared for battle. What they did not know was that an armed escort of three English warships, commanded by Captain Edward Barlow on the thirty-six-gun *Sceptre*, now accompanied the fleet.

In an attempt to appease the Grand Mogul after Henry Every's brutish attack on the *Ganj-i-Sawai*, the East India Company had promised fleet protection in return for continued trading rights with India. Early on August 14, 1697, under a red flag of piracy, the *Adventure Galley* sailed toward the fleet. With the wind easing off, Kidd ordered his men to row toward one of the pilgrim ships, fire a broadside, and cut her off from the rest of the fleet.

Captain Barlow raised the flag of the East India Company. Realizing it did not deter the attack, Barlow ordered men to lower the longboats and tow the *Sceptre* in closer to the *Adventure Galley*. Barlow then ordered his gunners to fire at will and positioned men aloft shouting threats and firing rifles. Kidd, thinking the *Sceptre* more heavily armed than she actually was, lost his nerve and retreated.

The situation for William Kidd got worse. His ship was damaged and leaking water, his supplies were lost or ruined, and his men were in an increasing mutinous mood. He set course for the port town of Karwar on the southern tip of India. Along the way he and his crew attempted to capture numerous vessels they encountered, with little success.

Eventually, one Indian trading vessel traveling off the coast of Malabar (India) fell into their trap. The ship, crewed by Indians but flying English flags and captained by Thomas Parker as well as a Portuguese officer by the name of Don Antonio, received the brunt of the men's frustrations. While Captain Kidd on the *Adventure Galley* questioned Parker and Don Antonio, Kidd's men bound many of the Indian crew and hoisted them aloft. They proceeded to torture the prisoners as they swung from ropes, beating them with cutlasses and demanding to know where any money was hidden aboard their ship. The men managed to find one hundred pieces of eight on the trading ship, stole coffee and sugar, then set the ship and Indian crew free. Captain Parker and Antonio unwillingly remained with the *Adventure Galley* as the new navigator and translator.

News of the attack on the pilgrim fleet and, more important, on a ship flying English colors, not to mention the kidnapping of Parker and Antonio, reached the city of Karwar well before the *Adventure Galley* on September 3, 1697. Captain Kidd vehemently denied the accusations but kept the two men locked aboard and guarded while taking on water and galley wood.

The East India Company now considered him a pirate for attacking a ship flying English colors. Many of Kidd's men had the same opinion. They had signed on as privateers, not pirates. A quarter of the crew deserted. When Captain Barlow landed at Surat, he reported Kidd's attack on the fleet. The viceroy of Goa, on the west coast of India, dispatched two Portuguese warships to capture the *Adventure Galley*, but Kidd managed to escape. Needing to again careen and repair the ship, Kidd found a perfect spot at the Maldive Islands of southwest India.

Kidd's men were now beyond any civilized actions. The villagers were forced to work on careening the vessel. The pirates broke up fishing boats for firewood and continually raped the island women. When the ship's cooper (the man who made and maintained barrels) wandered off alone, some natives captured him, slitting his throat.

In retaliation the pirates burned the natives' houses and slaughtered most of the men.

Kidd's authority over his crew hung by a thread. When they encountered an East India Company ship, the *Loyal Captain*, Kidd's crew voted to capture her. Captain Kidd refused the plan. When his men decided to lower the longboats and take the ship anyway, it took all of his blustering threats of revenge plus his strong will to get them to back down.

With no prize money and little food for the crew, it was only a matter of time before things fell apart. On October 30, 1697, they spotted a Dutch ship. The men voted to attack. The Dutch being an ally of the English, Captain Kidd refused. William Moore, one of the ship's gunners, was on deck grinding a chisel. He continued to suggest various scenarios for attacking the Dutch.

Kidd, after he ordered the men to stand down, considered Moore's suggestions as mutiny. According to trial testimony Kidd called Moore "a lousy dog." Moore shot back, "If I am a lousy dog, you have made me so; you have brought me to ruin and many more."

Never able to keep his temper in check, Kidd screamed, "I have ruined you, you dog?" He grabbed a wooden bucket encircled with iron hoops and smashed it against Moore's right temple. Moore crumpled to the deck and was taken below to the surgeon. It was quickly confirmed that Kidd had fractured Moore's skull. He died the next day.

Emotions running rampant aboard his vessel, Kidd made the decision to attack whatever ship they came across for prize money to placate his crew. Kidd cruised up and down the Indian coast and seized Dutch, Moorish, and Portuguese vessels, landing at various ports and selling the ill-gotten gains. Kidd sold enough cargo to share out sufficient money to appease his men.

One ploy privateers and pirates used to lure their prey to them became the trick of national flags. Ships carried a number of flags from all nations along with the nations' identification passports, also known simply as passes. Whether a privateer or pirate, crews would fly whatever flag was needed to get close enough to capture their target. In November, Kidd encountered the *Rouparelle*, a Dutch ship with an Indian crew. With the *Adventure Galley* flying the French flag, the *Rouparelle* approached cautiously. When Captain Michael Dickers came aboard the *Adventure Galley*, he was met by one of Kidd's French crewmen pretending to be the captain. Captain Dickers, hoping to save his ship, showed his French pass. This meant though the ship was flying Dutch colors, it was in fact a French-owned cargo. Kidd was ecstatic. This was his first legitimate seizure. Renaming the ship the *November*, Kidd released her crew onto a longboat and kept the *November* as an additional pirate ship. Keeping the French pass as proof of legitimate privateering, Captain Kidd sold the cargo to an East India Company employee known to fence pirate loot. Kidd once again had enough to pay his crew.

It wasn't until January 30, 1698, that Kidd took his one and only rich prize. Off Cochin, India, a ship came into sight. The forty-ton ship *Quedah Merchant*, with only ten guns, was owned by Muklis Khan, a wealthy Surat merchant and member of the Grand Mogul Aurangzeb's court. Once again Captain Kidd hoisted a French flag atop his mainmast to draw his prey closer, with the *November* blocking any escape. Seeing Kidd's French flag, Captain John Wright of the *Quedah Merchant* raised his own French ensign flag. Presuming he would be allowed safe passage, he went aboard the *Adventure Galley*, producing his own French pass.

Captain Wright was shocked when Kidd informed him they were English privateers and were seizing not only his cargo but the ship as well. Her cargo of silk, opium, sugar, iron, saltpeter, and calico was sold at Quilon (Kallam), a seaport city in Kerala, India. Even with Kidd keeping a chest of fine cloth for himself, the cargo yielded each crewman £7,000 to £12,000 ($3.5 million to $6 million) per shared booty.

Now with a fleet of three ships, Kidd and his men continued to attack vessels along the coast of India. Familiar with the weather patterns of the area, by late February 1698 Kidd knew the monsoon winds would very soon reverse course to a continual southwesterly direction. He had only a matter of days to leave the Indian Ocean or his fleet would be stranded in the area until sometime in October. Captain Kidd had to move quickly. The *Adventure Galley* was taking on water at such a rate that their captive Indian seamen, working the ship's pumps around the clock, could hardly keep the ship from sinking. The ship was in such bad shape that Kidd had men securely tie cables around the hull to keep the vessel from splitting apart. The three ships set course for St. Mary's Island. There Captain Kidd, who was originally commissioned to capture any and all known pirates, did no such thing. Instead he and his crew spent months enjoying their company. When Kidd was ready to depart once again, many of his crew chose to remain on the island.

Incensed that the East India Company could not keep its guarantee of protection against English pirates attacking in his domain, the Grand Mogul once again shut down all trade and imprisoned all English citizens in his territories. . The Grand Mogul did not differentiate one English pirate from another. He knew Henry Every's name from the testimonies of the rape survivors from the *Ganj-i-Sawai*. Therefore, he refused to discuss or allow any business with England until Henry Every was caught and executed

With all revenue streams stopped, the owners of the East India Company, many of them members of Parliament, petitioned the king. To quell the heightened pirate attacks, on December 8, 1698, King William III signed the Proclamation of Clemency, also known as the Act of Grace. The proclamation gave all English pirates sailing across the known world until July 1699 to surrender without any ramification. Two men were specifically excluded by name from the Act of Grace: Henry Every, alias Benjamin Bridgman, and William Kidd. The government hoped that by apprehending one or both men they would be able to satisfy the Grand Mogul's demands.

In November 1698, the same month that Captain Kidd and his men sailed from St. Mary's for the American colonies, the English government issued orders to all colonial governors. They were to actively pursue and capture Captain William Kidd for acts of piracy. Kidd learned of this only when he attempted to land at St. Thomas in the Caribbean. Realizing the danger he was now in, Kidd sailed the *Quedah Merchant*, renamed the *Adventure Prize*, to the friendly island of Hispaniola. Knowing he could not sail such an obviously exotic vessel to the American colonies, Captain Kidd purchased the sloop *St. Antonio* and left the *Adventure Prize* anchored at the island.

With more of his men choosing to remain on Hispaniola, Kidd sailed with a mere twenty-man crew first to New Jersey, then Long Island, stopping at Gardiner Island. He deposited much of his personal share of treasure with John Gardiner for safekeeping. Kidd then made arrangements for his wife to join him.

Since he had the two French passes in his possession, Kidd did not consider himself a pirate. He was therefore able to convince himself and his wife he would be cleared of all charges. Kidd conveniently forgot he had attacked at least two ships flying English ensign flags. He also presumed the Earl of Bellomont would vouch for his actions.

Kidd's wife hired the prominent lawyer James Emmot, a fellow member of Trinity Church. He traveled to Boston, Massachusetts, to represent Kidd's interests. What the three of them didn't know was that the Earl of Bellomont viewed Emmot as a Jacobite, a close friend of Benjamin Fletcher, and therefore Bellomont's personal enemy. Bellomont informed Emmot that Kidd would be promised a pardon, "if indeed Kidd was as innocent of piracy as he had claimed." With that reassurance Kidd went to Boston and met the Earl of Bellomont on July 3, 1699. Kidd professed his innocence to the charges of piracy and handed Bellomont the two sets of French passes. As a bribe, Kidd broadly hinted to Bellomont of his vast treasure that he had buried on Gardiner Island.

Newspapers and broadsheets were now printing daily stories of many well-known pirates of the day who were raiding the seas. Many attacks that were perpetrated by those others were being attributed to Kidd. The public, both in the colonies and in England, was obsessed with the news stories of "the Bloody Pirate Kidd."

Captain William Kidd was formally arrested on July 25, 1699, and sent to the stone prison in Boston. As soon as Kidd was chained in his cell, the Earl of Bellomont, governor of Massachusetts and New York, sent men several times to Gardiner Island to locate Kidd's buried treasure. They could not find any hint that treasure was indeed buried there.

Kidd's trial was ordered to take place in England. He arrived in London on April 11, 1700, and languished in the Old Bailey gaol for a year before his trial date was set. During that year Kidd corresponded with the House of Commons, stating that he could not be fairly tried, as his proof of innocence, the French passes, were not available to him.

Members of the English government saw Kidd's capture as an excellent opportunity not only to placate the Grand Mogul, but also to help with their own political aspirations. In an attempt to impeach Lord Somers and Lord Oxford from Parliament, warring political parties used Kidd's trial as proof that the men were part of Kidd's "ill gotten adventure into piracy." The impeachment attempt failed.

In all fairness to him, the Earl of Bellomont did indeed send Kidd's French passes to the House of Commons. The passes were recorded as being received, but somehow the passes were conveniently misplaced and never produced at the trial.

On May 8, 1701, Captain Kidd was formally charged with two crimes: the murder of William Moore and acts of piracy on the high seas. He was not permitted legal representation and had to cross-examine witnesses himself. All witnesses with favorable accounts of Kidd's actions had their testimonies dismissed by the judges. The judges viewed the witnesses as men of dubious character and, as a result, completely unreliable sources.

During the trial the English government needed to have public opinion on its side. Even if the accusation of murder of a crewman was true, it was a rare thing indeed for a ship's captain to be publicly charged with the crime.

Kidd continued to argue that although the ship was Dutch crewed, by evidence of the French passes, the ship and cargo were consigned to England's enemy France and a legitimate seizure. The king's prosecutor insisted that if the passes were the only proof the court would accept as proof of Kidd's innocence, then they needed to be produced immediately. Not being able to produce the passes as evidence on his own behalf, Captain Kidd was found guilty of piracy and murder. The trial ended on May 9, 1701, with the judges ordering his death by hanging.

Hanging a pirate was a newsworthy public event. On May 23, 1701, Captain William Kidd was escorted to the execution dock at Wapping, a district of east London that borders the Thames. A huge crowd gathered to see the end of this infamous man.

Even his death did not go swiftly. Once the noose tightened around his neck, the hangman's rope snapped. Kidd dropped to the ground, breaking the scaffold. The executioner could find only a rickety ladder to continue with the execution. Dragging Kidd to the top rung of the ladder, he tied a new rope around the pirate's neck. Before the executioner pushed the ladder out from under him, Captain Kidd once again professed his innocence. The new rope held tight.

Captain William Kidd's body was tarred and sent to Tilbury Point on the Thames. There, wrapped in chains, his body was placed into an iron gibbet (a type of cage), where it hung for years as a warning to all who would consider a life of piracy.

Three days after the execution an English envoy set sail. The envoy met the Grand Mogul, informing him of the death of William Kidd, a pirate now far more notorious than Henry Every. Placated, the Grand Mogul Aurangzeb ordered the release of all English prisoners and allowed trade negotiations to resume with the

East India Company. The Grand Mogul never received his promised financial compensation.

In 1911 American historian Ralph Paine was researching documents in England for his manuscript *The Book of Buried Treasure*. He had access to all the boxes of files stored in the Public Records Office in London. There, Paine found the original French pass issued for the *Quedah Merchant*.

CHAPTER NINE

John Quelch and Crewmates

JOHN QUELCH AND HIS CAPTURED CREWMATES HAD THE DUBIOUS honor of being the first men to be placed officially on trial for piracy outside of England. Prior to that date all trials were governed by the Offence at Sea Act of 1536. It stated that all cases of piracy had to be heard by the Lord High Admiral and four common law judges appointed by the Lord High Chancellor, and therefore take place in England. With piracy on the rise all over the world, this created quite a burden on colonial governors. They were required not only to house and feed the accused men, but also to send them to England to be put on trial, which became extremely costly.

To lessen that burden, in 1700 the Act for the More Effectual Suppression of Piracy became law. It enabled the vice-admiralty courts in English-held territories to hold trials and authorized the use of the death penalty. Since the act pertained to piracy under the umbrella of the English Naval Admiralty Law, one stipulation was that those individuals sentenced to death had to be executed on or near the watermark, meaning between low and high tides.

In 1702 a consortium of Boston's leading citizens and merchants—Charles Hobby, Colonel Nicholas Paige, William Clarke, Benjamin Gallop, and John Colman—purchased the newly built brigantine *Charles*. Their intention was to hire her out as a privateer for profit, to attack French shipping off the coast of Acadia and Newfoundland in Canadian waters. On July 13, 1703, Joseph Dudley, the Crown's appointed governor of the Massachusetts Bay and New Hampshire Provinces, commissioned the *Charles* for such a voyage. It was also widely known to the citizenry throughout New England that the majority of colonial governmental officials turned a blind eye to privateering without a license as long as each official received his cut of the profits.

With the *Charles* anchored at Marblehead, Massachusetts, and waiting to sail, her captain, Daniel Plowman, became severely ill. He sent a letter on August 1, 1703, to the owners of the *Charles*. In the missive he informed them of his illness and inability to sail the vessel. Plowman added that one or more of them should travel immediately to Marblehead and make plans to sail the ship back to Boston and unload all the guns and supplies. Plowman urged them not to simply send the ship out with a new captain and with the same crew, as the owners first suggested. He firmly believed the endeavor "will not do with these people." Plowman was positive the ship's crew was up to no good. His intuition was right.

Before the owners could act on his advice, the crew of the *Charles*, headed by Anthony Holding, locked Plowman in his cabin and took command of the ship. At that moment John Quelch boarded as ship's navigator. The men convinced Quelch to become their captain.

Quelch ordered the men to raise anchor. He sailed the *Charles*, now a pirate ship, out of Marblehead Harbor and past Marblehead Rock, Cat Island, and Halfway Rock; then he set the ship's course southward. Once out in open waters, the men dumped Plowman overboard. Whether the poor man was dead or alive at the time is not recorded in trial records.

The owners of the *Charles*, not able to obtain any information on the vessel's movements, sent circulars throughout the West Indies for any news on the whereabouts of their ship. They received no information from their inquiries. Being an educated man, Quelch knew there was little gold to be gotten from merely attacking French shipping. So he charted a course for the rich South Atlantic area, where gold mines were known to exist. The *Charles* reached Brazil on November 15, 1703.

Without the letter of marque that declared them legal privateers, Quelch and crew began attacking ships. Through the next three months, ending on February 17, 1704, they seized nine Portuguese vessels. Their haul was considerable. It consisted of gold and silver coins valued at over £1,000 ($500,000), ammunition, small firearms, gold dust weighing over one hundred pounds, cloth, silks, sugar, rum, and food provisions, in addition to a number of black and Indian slaves.

With their booty securely aboard, the men set sail back to Marblehead, Massachusetts. The reasoning behind the decision to return to Marblehead, the port they originally departed from when they turned pirate, was never given.

The *Boston News-Letter* was the first newspaper to be published in the Massachusetts Bay area. Only its fifth edition, the May 15–22, 1704, issue reported that "the *Charles* Arrived at Marblehead, Capt. Quelch in the Brigantine that Capt. Plowman went out in, and said to come from New Spain and have made a good voyage."

This was not an unusual announcement for the newspaper to print. With piracy becoming more prevalent in the 1700s, the *Boston News-Letter* began to publish the names of all men departing on a legitimate ship. If mid-voyage they were forced to join a pirate crew, the "forced notices" would be used in their trials as evidence of possible innocence.

Upon arrival in Marblehead, the crew immediately dispersed throughout the cities and towns of Massachusetts and Rhode Island. Quelch claimed that the treasure they brought back was from a wrecked ship they discovered in the Indies. Though the residents of Marblehead knew the ship was originally bound northward, the common citizenry still considered piracy a viable profession. Pirates brought needed money into the pockets of uninfluential merchants and tradesmen. The townspeople kept Quelch's secret to themselves.

Prior to the early 1700s, it had been the practice of wealthy merchants to privately outfit a ship as a privateer. Depending upon unforeseen circumstances, the merchants would incur either a monetary profit or monetary loss from the venture. However, when their pocketbooks were subject to severe losses from pirates, more so than simply foul weather, the idea of syndicates and institutions emerged to minimize individual loses.

Global trade helped spur the creation of the Bank of England and the insurance firm Lloyds of London. The continued success of monopoly business ventures such as the East India Company had an enormous sway on the political and judicial decisions of the time, especially concerning pirates.

Having read of the ship's return, two of the ship's owners, John Colman and William Clarke, filed a complaint on May 23, 1704, with Paul Dudley, attorney general of the Massachusetts province. He just happened to be the son of Massachusetts governor Joseph Dudley.

Not only was John Colman an investor in the *Charles*, he was the appointed colonial agent for Prince George of Denmark, consort to Queen Anne of England. Prince George had been appointed in England as Lord of the High Admiralty. As such, Prince George was automatically entitled to a large percentage of all profits received from captured cargo and ships brought into Boston Harbor. Colman's job was to make sure Prince George received that money and received it promptly.

On May 24, Lieutenant Governor Thomas Povey issued a proclamation to all officers, civil and military, to apprehend the suspected pirates of the *Charles* and secure any and all treasure they had upon their person. Povey accused them "of importing a considerable Quantity of Gold dust which they are violently suspected to have gotten and obtained by Felony and Piracy, from some of Her Majesty's Friends and Allies."

Along with John Quelch, the proclamation listed the forty-five suspected pirates by name:

James Austin

John Breck

Denis Carter

John Carter

Daniel Chevalle

Daniel Churley

John Clifford

Gabriel Davis

John Dorothy

Nicholas Dunbar

Thomas Farrington

Paul Giddins

John Harwood

Anthony Holding

Joseph Hutnot

Charles James

Isaac Johnson

William Jones

Charles King

Francis King

John King

John Lambert

Richard Lawrence

Nicholas Lawson

John Miller

George Norton

James Parret

James Pattison

George Peirse

Benjamin Perkins

Erasmus Peterson

John Pitman

Matthew Primer

John Quittance

William Rayner

Nicholas Richardson

Peter Roach

Christopher Scudamore

Richard Thurbar

John Templeton

John Way

Joseph Wells

William Whiting

William Wiles

Daniel Wormal

The hunt for the men of the *Charles* was on, encompassing every colony of New England. It was proclaimed in every town and village that anyone who received a portion of the seized cargo must turn it over to the authorities or be prosecuted as a pirate themselves. Hundreds of coins, fabrics, and goods were brought to local gaols, for fear of neighbors turning in their own neighbors. Reward proclamations for the men's capture were posted in taverns, tap houses, and brothels.

A Commission of Inquiry was formed on June 6, 1704. Its members were Samuel Sewall, acting chief justice of the Superior Court; Nathaniel Byfield, judge of the Court of the Admiralty; and Paul Dudley, attorney general.

A Salem, Massachusetts, customs officer, Samuel Wakefield, sent a message to the commission informing them that several of Quelch's pirates had boarded the ship *Larramore Galley*, captained by Thomas Larramore. The alleged pirates John Carter, Charles James, Charles King, John King, Joseph Wells, and Daniel Wormal were attempting an escape. Judges Sewall and Byfield rode to Salem. They appointed Major Stephen Sewall, clerk of the Inferior Court, who happened to be Judge Sewall's brother, to gather twenty militia volunteers, acquire two ships, and apprehend the escaping pirates. The *Larramore Galley* was quickly seized without any loss of life. The fugitives were brought to Boston Prison, instead of the gaol, to stand trial.

Unaware of the proclamation, so fearing no reprisals for his actions, the 38-year-old John Quelch traveled to Boston from Marblehead to conduct business. He intended to purchase his own vessel and return to privateering.

However, first he went to his favorite tap house, Noah's Ark on Boston's Northside, and ordered a tankard of hot flip. Flip was a very popular New England drink that consisted of strong beer mixed with sugar and a dash of rum and nutmeg. A hot poker would be inserted into the tankard, heating the drink until it frothed.

Quelch was shocked when Paul Dudley, the attorney general of Massachusetts himself, with dragoons and local militia in tow, entered the tap house. They arrested Quelch on charges of murder, piracy, and illegally importing goods into the colony. Immediately placing him in irons, the constables dragged Quelch from the tap house through the winding streets of Boston and threw him into prison.

As was allowed at that time, all of the trials of the *Charles* crew took place in the Star Tavern, on Hanover Street, Boston. The tavern was temporarily turned into a makeshift courtroom. All the pirates on the *Charles* gave their testimonies in the Star Tavern.

On June 9, 1704, Captain Thomas Larramore became the first to stand trial. Captain Larramore was accused of turning pirate as soon as he took money from the accused pirates and raised anchor. He was condemned to death by hanging. On June 11 he was led to Boston Wharf and taken by boat across the Charles River, to his waiting gallows on Nix's Mate Island. There he was unceremoniously hanged.

On June 13, 1704, thirty-three of the pirates listed in Povey's proclamation were brought to trial for piracy, murder, and transporting illegal goods into the country.

John Clifford, James Parret, and Matthew Primer turned king's evidence against the others and escaped the hangman's noose. John Templeton was discovered to be 14, and he had served only as cabin boy on the *Charles.* He was acquitted. The remainder of the *Charles*'s crew managed to escape capture.

Part of the men's defense hinged on the fact that the crew of the *Charles* had no knowledge that Portugal and England had signed a peace treaty on May 16, 1703. This, in the eyes of the law, rendered them pirates, not privateers, for their attacks on the new ally of England.

Though it was customary at that time not to grant permission for legal counsel, the court did allow the lawyer James Meinzie to represent John Quelch. The *Boston News-Letter* reported that, despite Meinzie's best efforts, and an excellent and convincing closing argument, Quelch was found guilty of all charges and sentenced to hang.

All the other accused men from the *Charles* were found guilty of the crimes with which they were charged. As was a common custom of the time, even if a man was found guilty, the judge had the legal right to grant him a reprieve. Not wanting to create a bloodbath, the judge used "the benefit of clergy," an avenue of repentance, to reprieve all but seven men. Pardons were even granted to the men of Quelch's crew who had not been apprehended.

The executions of John Quelch, John Lambert, Christopher Scudamore, John Miller, Erasmus Peterson, Peter Roach, and Francis King, however, were set for June 30.

From June 11 to June 30 the prisoners were barraged daily by ministers, especially the prestigious Cotton Mather, in an attempt to get them to truly repent before God and especially the public. On Friday, June 30, the condemned men were marched through the streets of Boston behind the Silver Oar, the emblem of the Court of the Admiralty. As they were led through the town of Boston guarded by forty musketeers, the provost marshal, and town constables, two ministers followed along, one of them being Cotton Mather.

Hundreds turned out in the streets to see the spectacle of the fierce pirates being marched to their deaths. The crowds watched as the men were ferried across the harbor to Nix's Mate Island. There a gallows had been constructed to simultaneously hang all seven.

In Judge Sewall's diary, he estimates that 100 to 150 boats and canoes were on the river that day watching the executions.

The seven men were lined up on the gallows. The condemned men were allowed, and even expected, to address the crowds. The ministers hoped they would ask for mercy and be a great deterrent for any young man thinking of joining the pirate way.

John Lambert continued to profess his innocence. To the pleasure of the ministers, he asked, "Lord, forgive my Soul," and he "desired all men to beware of Bad Company." Christopher Scudamore, John Miller, and Peter Roach had little to say. Erasmus Peterson felt his execution was a grave injustice, stating, "It is very hard for so many men's lives to be taken away for a little gold." Peterson asked the executioner to do his job well and put him out of his misery as soon as possible.

John Quelch stepped forward and, removing his hat, bowed to the waiting crowd. He stated, "I am not afraid of Death, I am not afraid of the Gallows, but I am afraid of what follows; I am afraid of a Great God, and a Judgment to Come." Composing himself, Quelch added to the crowd, "I desire to be informed for what I am here. I am condemned only upon circumstances. They [men] should also take care how they brought money into New England, to be hanged for it."

At the last minute, with the noose around his neck, Francis King received a reprieve and was escorted off the scaffold.

John Lambert's wife paid to be allowed to quietly inter her husband in the family cemetery plot that evening, but the other five bodies were placed in gibbets until their flesh rotted away to mere bone.

Before their bodies were cold, the colonial officials dispersed the pirates' booty. The owner of the Star Tavern received a generous amount of money "for entertainment of the commissioners during court proceeding." Governor Joseph Dudley received an unrecorded share. Attorney General Paul Dudley received £36 ($18,000). Major Sewall, Captain Turner, and their volunteers each received £132.50 ($67,250). Judge Sewall and his Commission of Inquiry received £25.70 each ($14,250). Sheriff Dryer of New Hampshire received £5 ($2,500). The executioner received £2 ($1,000). Thomas Bernard received 40 shillings (£2.00; $364.00) for erecting the four gibbets.

Reverend Cotton Mather, Queen's Counsel, the prison counsel, marshals, and prison guards all received undisclosed amounts of money. In total £726.19.0 ($363,275) was disbursed.

Sometime in 1706, a mere 788 ounces (49 pounds, 4 ounces) of gold dust was sent to the English Crown and Prince George. The remaining amount of treasure John Quelch and his crew acquired through the sale of slaves, spices, and exotic goods had not been recorded.

After Captain Quelch's execution, Reverend Cotton Mather published a treatise entitled *Instructions to the Living, from the Condition of the Dead*.

CHAPTER TEN

Samuel "Black Sam" Bellamy

SAMUEL "BLACK SAM" BELLAMY IS WELL KNOWN IN THE FOLKLORE of Cape Cod, Massachusetts, as a tragic romantic figure and a notable pirate.

Neither of the two surviving pirates from the *Whydah* shipwreck mentioned why Bellamy chose to sail his treasure ship to Cape Cod one fateful night. However, to the locals of Cape Cod it made perfect sense, and through the years they created folklore about him that is very much alive to this day.

To hear it told, it happened on a spring night in Billingsgate, Massachusetts, in 1715. The story begins with the 26-year-old Samuel Bellamy meeting a 16-year-old girl named Mary Hallett in the taproom of a tavern. They fall madly and deeply in love. Her wealthy farming parents, though they approve of him, do not allow her to marry a penniless sailor. Sam Bellamy vows to go to sea and return with enough wealth to impress Mary's father and bless their marriage.

While he is away Mary discovers she is pregnant. She secretly has the baby, but is discovered hiding in a barn with her dead baby in her arms. Billingsgate is a very religious Puritan town, and the clergy drag Mary into the town square to publicly whip her and throw her into the town gaol. She is slated to go on trial for her baby's murder. While waiting for the trial date to be announced, realizing Samuel is not returning to her, Mary has a psychotic breakdown. Now out of her mind, the officials take pity on her and sign her release. She becomes a recluse, living in a dilapidated shack on a stark plateau of land overlooking the Atlantic Ocean. For the rest of her life she is known as "Goody Hallett" or the "Sea Witch of Billingsgate." The town, situated at the northern end of Eastham, is later renamed Wellfleet. Today, there is a meadow in the Wellfleet area known as Goody Hallett Meadow.

Folklore aside, Samuel Bellamy was born to tenant farmers Stephen and Elizabeth Pain Bellamy on March 18, 1689, in the small rural village of Hittisleigh, Devon, England. Bellamy grew up at the time when burgeoning capitalism found its way into the rural farmlands of England. For centuries country estates allowed their tenant farmers common open grazing lands. Slowly English lords began to enclose their lands into private estates.

The practice of wealthy lords and merchants purchasing medieval tenancy rights or simply ignoring a tenant's request to renew land leases helped create those breathtaking aristocratic estates. However, the act of enclosing the land created continual poverty amongst the once prosperous tenant farmers. If they wished to live on their land, they were required to pay rent for that privilege to the new landowners. Families raised livestock and grew vegetables, not to provide for their own table, but to generate enough money to pay their tenant rents. It became a common practice for entire families to hire themselves out as laborers to make enough money, so as not to get thrown out of their cottages. This practice sweeping through rural England perpetuated a growing hatred among the general populace for the wealthy and entitled. Bellamy grew up under these harsh conditions.

As soon as he was old enough, Bellamy, like other boys across the farmlands of England, left for a new start in a city or port town. When the War of the Spanish Succession broke out in 1701 he had just turned 13. We don't know if he was press-ganged or willingly signed onto a naval ship or merchantman. However, by the time the Peace of Utrecht was signed in 1712, the 24-year-old Bellamy was a skilled seaman, out of a job, and broke.

Bellamy arrived at Eastham, Massachusetts, near Cape Cod, in 1714 or 1715, looking for new opportunities. Finding none in the immediate area, he traveled to Boston. There he became fast friends with Paulgrave Williams, a 39-year-old silversmith, husband, and father of two young boys.

Coming from an influential Rhode Island family, Williams would not seem the type to need or want to go into the pirating trade. His father, John, was the attorney general of Rhode Island and a wealthy merchant. The family split their time between a Boston mansion and estates in Newport and Block Island. They traveled in elite social circles. Paulgrave's mother, Anna Alcock, was the daughter of a Harvard-trained physician and a descendent of the Plantagenet kings of England.

Paulgrave was 11 years old when his father died and his entire life changed. His mother married their legal executor and friend, Robert Guthrie. Guthrie, a Scottish exile, moved the family from Boston to permanently live at the estate on Block Island, Narragansett Bay, Rhode Island.

Guthrie's father, a fierce Scottish nationalist and preacher, had been executed by the English. The surviving members of the Guthrie family were tried for treason and banished from the country. They were sent with other Scottish prisoners to New England as indentured servants to the ironworks at Lynn and Braintree, Massachusetts. In time, quite a few of the Scots were able to relocate to Block Island and become part of a community of organized crime especially targeting the English.

Robert Guthrie moved his new family into an atmosphere that introduced Paulgrave Williams into a world of money launderers, smugglers, and black marketers operating throughout the entire New England area. Williams's older sister, Mary, married Edward Sands, a personal friend of Captain William Kidd. They even hid some of

Kidd's wealth while he was on the run from the law. His younger sister, Elizabeth, and her husband, Thomas Paine, also friends of Kidd, were implicated in Kidd's evasion of the authorities. Thomas Paine was the nephew of the retired pirate Thomas Paine the Elder, known in his old age as a buyer and seller of pirate plunder.

With Williams's money and influence and Bellamy's sailing knowledge, they realized the potential in purchasing a ship and trying their luck at sea. Paulgrave now simply preferred to be called Paul. Samuel went either by Sam or, as his friends called him, Black Sam. The nickname originated from Bellamy's refusal to wear the fashionable powdered wigs of the time. He simply pulled back his long black hair and tied it with a black satin ribbon. Flaunting the sumptuary laws of the time, Bellamy, a tall man, dressed in the finer clothes of the aristocracy, refusing to bend to the laws prohibiting him from wearing specific fabrics or colors.

On July 13, 1715, a Spanish treasure fleet of eleven vessels sailed out of Havana, Cuba, on its way to Cádiz, Spain. Since the war had for many years prevented any of the treasure fleets from sailing, the ships were carrying an unusually large amount. They also set sail dangerously late in the season. On Friday, July 19, the weather turned against them.

By midnight the fleet fought against hurricane-force winds of one hundred miles per hour. With the wind and waves fierce, the treasure ships were blown toward the treacherous Florida coast. The reefs became unavoidable. The crews knew there was no escaping death. Having sailed a few hours ahead of the fleet, only the *El Grifon* escaped unscathed.

When news of sunken Spanish treasure ships finally reached Boston, the two men decided they would indeed set sail and go into the "wrecking trade." With Sam Bellamy as captain and Paul Williams his quartermaster, and with a limited crew, they intended to salvage the sunken vessels for the lost wealth lying on the seafloor. By the time they reached the Florida area in January 1716, it was littered with ships and canoes crewed by brutish men with the very same intentions. Only a few scattered coins were discovered among them all before a Spanish war fleet arrived from Havana, Cuba, determined to drive them away.

Bellamy and Williams sailed to Central America and the Bay of Honduras. At Campeche in southeastern Mexico, they found the few surviving English loggers, nicknamed Baymen, whose illegal camp had been attacked by the Spanish militia. For fear of another attack, the Baymen were eager to leave the Campeche logging camp any way they could. The loggers signed onto Bellamy's ship.

As neither Bellamy nor Williams had any illusions they were anything other than pirates, they sold their original ship and purchased two piragua canoes to begin mounting their attacks. The piragua, very popular at the time, was a two-masted flat-bottom sailing canoe.

A Dutch vessel, captained by John Cornelison, became their first capture. As the crew plundered the ship, they forced a 34-year-old crewman, Peter Cornelius Hoof, to remain with them. He had two options: turn pirate or die right then and there. Hoof's extensive knowledge of the islands and waterways along the southern Caribbean Sea was needed to fulfill their plans. Grudgingly, he agreed.

The next ship they seized was an English sloop, commanded by a Captain Young, sailing in the Bay of Honduras. While their men ransacked the sloop (a one-masted sailboat), Williams and Bellamy had their piragua canoes tied along the vessel's hull and forced Captain Young to sail them back toward Cuba in search of prey.

After seeing the horrendous condition of the Baymen in the logging camps and the conditions of crews aboard the captured ships, Bellamy's hatred expanded. It now encompassed the landed gentry, but also ship owners, wealthy merchants, and captains who made life hell for all mariners. Bellamy proposed to his crewmates that they should act as Robin Hood and his band. They would plunder anything on the water they could from rich merchants and distribute the wealth to all the poor seamen they encountered. His men heartily agreed.

Off the coast of Cuba, the privateering fleet of Henry Jennings, captain of the *Barsheba*, along with Charles Vane of the *Mary* and Samuel Liddell on the *Cocoa Nut*, spotted Bellamy's ship and bore down to attack. Seeing a rapidly approaching fleet of ships all flying English flags, Bellamy and Williams did not realize pirates were aboard.

Bellamy ordered his crew of forty men to fill both piragua canoes with all their plunder. The men abandoned ship and rowed to shore. From the hidden mangroves the pirates watched the fleet's actions and realized the visitors were not militiamen. Waiting until evening, Bellamy and crew sailed the piragua canoes up to the *Barsheba* and hailed the captain. Pirate captains Sam Bellamy, Paul Williams, Henry Jennings, and Charles Vane met for the first time and became fast friends. They remained in the area of Bahía Honda, a sheltered, secluded anchorage on the Cuban coast, drinking and collecting water and wood.

Spotting a French frigate, the *St. Marie*, far off in the distance, Bellamy and crew agreed to help Jennings and Vane capture the vessel and divide the spoils. Liddell on the *Cocoa Nut* refused to turn from privateer to pirate. He sailed away with other crewmen who shared the same opinion.

Bellamy's men—shirtless, carrying flintlocks and swords, screaming at the top of their lungs—rowed the two piragua canoes straight toward the *St. Marie*, towing the *Barsheba* and *Mary* behind them. The terrifying sight terrorized the Frenchmen. They surrendered without either side firing a shot.

Everything went according to plan until the arrival of the ten-gunned armed sloop *Marianne* of the infamous Captain Benjamin Hornigold (a.k.a. Hornygold).

Pirate historians agree that Hornigold, was one of the most revered pirates of his time. He was responsible for the creation of a large number of famous pirate captains. Men crewing on his ships were promoted to captaincy when deciding to keep a prized vessel. Hornigold needed competent men to sail ships as part of his fleet.

Edward Teach (a.k.a. Thach), who later became known as Blackbeard, was one such crewman.

Years before, Jennings and Hornigold had a previous falling out, with Jennings still harboring very raw feelings. As soon as Henry Jennings realized Hornigold was in the area, he forgot about the *St. Marie*. With Vane's vessel right behind him, Jennings changed course and gave chase. Alone with the captured French frigate, Bellamy and Williams saw their chance. They ordered their men to fill one of their piragua canoes as full of booty from the French vessel as fast as they could. They sailed away before the other two pirate vessels returned, rowing away with a haul of over 28,500 pieces of eight ($14.25 million). In 1716 the average merchant captain's annual salary came to a mere £65 ($32,500).

After the theft Bellamy and Williams met Hornigold off the coast of Cuba. Hornigold loved the idea that when Jennings wasn't looking, they had stolen his share of the treasure. Bellamy and Williams, along with their remaining crew, signed Hornigold's ship's articles, tied up their one piragua onto a fleet ship, and happily joined Hornigold.

Sailing along the western coast of Cuba hoping to encounter more prey, they met the French pirate Olivier La Bouche sailing on the *Postillion*. Hornigold, a loyal Englishman who refused to attack English ships, or those of her allies, was of the old breed of buccaneers. Bellamy and La Bouche felt they had no loyalty to any nation's corrupt systems. Somehow all the ships' crews came to an agreement, and Hornigold's pirate fleet added another ship. The arrangement did not last long.

With Hornigold's adamant refusal to seize Dutch or English ships, the pirates felt they needed a new leader. After the quartermaster of the *Marianne* called for a full fleet vote, it became clear that Hornigold was outnumbered. Out of respect for the man, they allowed him to sail away on the captured ship *Adventure* with twenty-six of his loyal men.

Bellamy now commanded 170 pirates. Bellamy's pirate crew was international. It consisted of English, Irish, Scottish, Welsh, Spanish, Dutch, Swedish, and French men, as well as Hendrick Quintor, a free black man of African and Dutch ancestry, and approximately thirty former black slaves. As the pirate fleet continued to seize ships and cargos, they also forced unwilling men with special skills to join their crews. Besides Peter Hoff, four such men were John Brown, a rigger; Richard Caverley, a navigator; Dr. James Ferguson, a surgeon; and Thomas Davis, a ship's carpenter. Davis was so distraught at his enslavement, begging constantly to be set free, that Bellamy vowed he would free him the moment they "found" another carpenter.

The fleet voted to set their sights along the coast of South America, making their way to the Caribbean Islands and capturing as many vessels as they could along the way. On November 9, 1716, without any resistance, the fleet seized the sloop *Bonetta*, a passenger ship sailing from Jamaica to Antigua. Bellamy assured the captain, Abijah Savage, that no harm would come to him or his crew.

Careening their fleet ships on the nearly deserted island of St. Croix, the pirates spent fifteen days aboard the *Bonetta*, using the vessel as their own. After taking all the supplies they needed from the *Bonetta*, including the clothing of the wealthy passengers, true to his word, Captain Bellamy informed Captain Savage that he was free to leave.

One passenger, a young boy 8 or 9 years of age named John King, had been pleading with Bellamy all fifteen days to allow him to join the pirate crew. To the profound relief of his mother, Bellamy and crew laughingly ignored the boy's pleas.

Exactly as the sumptuary laws wished to emphasize, it was obvious to all simply by looking at the boy's clothing that John King came from a well-to-do family. His clothes were made of the finest fabric, woven French silk stockings covered his legs, and he wore stylish leather heeled shoes attached with silver buckles.

When Bellamy gave the order to release the lines connecting the ships, a desperate John King announced he would kill himself. When his mother tried to restrain the boy, King grew more violent and threatened to kill his mother. At this point Bellamy and crew agreed to take him along. To his mother's horror, the boy swore loyalty to the pirates and agreed to add his name to the ship's articles. He boarded the *Marianne*, and the pirates released the *Bonetta*. Knowing it would not take long for news of their whereabouts to be broadcast, Bellamy ordered the fleet toward the Spanish Main.

When the *Bonetta* reached Antigua, Captain Savage reported the pirate attack and the horrific news about John King to the island governor: "He further saith, that one John King who was coming as a passenger with him from the said Island of Jamaica to the Island of Antigua deserted his sloop, and went with the Pirates and was so far from being forced or compelled thereto by them as the deponent could perceive or learn that he declared he would Kill himself if he was Restrained, and even threatened his Mother who was then on Board as a Passenger with the Deponent."

In November 1716 Bellamy captured the English ship *Sultana* with twenty-six guns. By vote, the pirates put Bellamy in command of the *Sultana* and chose Paul Williams as captain of the *Marianne*. At this point all the men felt nothing could stop them. They continued plundering ships along the way, taking cargo and seizing skilled men to add to their crews. They were able to capture the majority of their victims with little to no violence. When satisfied they had all they wished to plunder from a vessel, Bellamy's fleet would release the ship to continue on its voyage.

In late February 1717, the slave ship *Whydah*, named after the famous slave center on the African Gold Coast and commanded by Captain Lawrence Prince, left Jamaica bound for London. The vessel had eighteen mounted guns and a crew of fifty men. Her hull was full of precious cargo. The ship carried elephant tusks, gold dust, sugar, rum, slave profits of £20,000 ($10 million), indigo, and Jesuit's bark. Jesuit's bark is the bark of the Cinchona tree found in Peru. It is best known for its active ingredient, quinine, the only known cure at the time for the ravages of malaria.

The only course the *Whydah*'s navigator knew to reach London required the ship to pass through the Windward Passage between Cuba and Puerto Rico. In March 1717 the watch aboard the *Sultana* spied the *Whydah*. The pirate fleet gave chase. After being hounded for three days, Captain Prince realized escape was hopeless. He surrendered the *Whydah*.

With a picked crew, including young John King, Bellamy transferred to the *Whydah*, adding ten more guns to her deck, along with additional cannon shot, ammo, and grenades.

Pleased that Captain Prince did not put up a fight, Bellamy gave the *Sultana* to him, leaving an amount of cargo aboard that the pirates did not want. In addition, Bellamy personally handed Prince £20 ($10,000) in gold and silver coin "to bear his charges."

Before the *Sultana* was due to sail, Thomas Davis reminded Bellamy of his vow to release him. Bellamy agreed to do so only if the rest of the pirate fleet voted that Davis could leave. To Davis's dismay, they refused his request. Dejected and under armed guard, Davis boarded the *Whydah*. The pirates forced three unmarried crewmen of the *Whydah* to remain aboard. By now the pirates had over fifty forced men on their combined ships.

With over fifty-three ships captured in a one-year period and untold wealth aboard their ships, in early March of 1717 the 28-year-old Samuel Bellamy announced to his men, "Lads, we have gotten enough." Captain Bellamy was ready to depart for home. They all agreed to his plan. Before they set sail, Richard Nolan, Bellamy's quartermaster, counted out the coins they had captured. Under the watchful eye of the fleet quartermaster, Nolan carefully placed fifty pounds of silver and gold coins and a measured quantity of gold dust into separate leather bags, one for each pirate, and stored them below deck on the *Whydah*.

The pirates voted to sail up the eastern seaboard, seizing as many ships as they could. It was now springtime. After the long winter it was the best chance to catch ships loaded with cargo leaving the eastern colonies. It was agreed that if they were separated by inclement weather or unforeseen circumstances, the three ships would meet up at Damariscove Island in Maine.

During the North American campaign of the War of the Spanish Succession, attacking Frenchmen and Indians had burned down most of the settlements in Maine. The vessels could easily anchor undetected in a secluded area. The lush forests in that area could supply wood to refit their ship masts and make other needed repairs.

In early April, off the coast of South Carolina, the pirates seized a Boston-owned sloop commanded by a Captain Beer. While pirates plundered his vessel, Bellamy and Williams entertained the captain on the *Whydah*. Their attempts to convince Captain Beer to join the pirate fleet failed. After their crews took all the cargo they wanted, Bellamy and Williams intended on returning Beer to his ship. For whatever reason, the pirates voted to burn the vessel instead. With the majority vote against returning the ship, Bellamy sadly reported the news to Captain Beer. In the habit of writing daily in a journal, that evening Captain Beer transcribed Bellamy's comments:

Damn my Blood, says he. I am sorry they won't let you have your Sloop again, for I scorn to do any one a Mischief, when it is not for my Advantage; damn the sloop, we must sink her, and she might be of Use to you. Tho', damn ye, you are a sneaking Puppy, and so are all those who will submit to be governed by Laws which rich Men have made for their own Security, for the cowardly Whelps have not the Courage otherwise to defend what they get by their Knavery; but damn ye altogether: Damn them for a Pack of crafty

Rascals, and you, who serve them, for a Parcel of hen-hearted Numskuls. They vilify us, the Scoundrels do, when there is only this Difference, they rob the Poor under the Cover of Law, forsooth, and we plunder the Rich under the Protection of our own Courage; had you not better make One of us, than sneak after the Asses of those Villians for Employment?

When Captain Beer informed Bellamy his conscience would never allow him to break the laws of God or men and turn pirate, Bellamy continued his tirade:

Rascal, Damn ye, I am a free Prince, and I have as much Author-ity to make War on the whole World, as he who has a hundred Sail of Ships at Sea, and an Army of 100,000 Men in the Field; and this my Conscience tells me; but there is no arguing with such sniveling Puppies, who allow Superiors to kick them about Deck at Pleasure; and pin their Faith upon a Pimp of a Parson; a Squab, who neither practices nor believes what he puts upon the chuck-le-headed Fools he preaches to.

Captain Beer transferred onto the *Marianne* while he watched his ship burn and sink into the sea. Williams intended to land first at Block Island, Rhode Island, for a family reunion before sailing on to Massachusetts. His crewmates were pleased with his decision. It was common knowledge that Williams's family could help dispose of much of their booty for a fair price.

The two ships set sail under a deep April fog and soon were sep-arated. Bellamy sailed on and captured the *Agnes of Glasgow*, the *Ann Galley*, and the *Endeavor* along the way. It was decided to keep the *Ann Galley* as a storage ship, and after plundering the other vessels the pirates set them free.

After separating from Bellamy, Williams sailed up the Chesa-peake. His ship was not as fortified as the *Whydah* to take on many vessels. With his crew growing restless, Williams attacked the first ship they sighted, the *Tryal* captained by John Lucas, and captured her. When the winds unexpectedly increased in strength, the *Tryal* managed to escape. Fearing she would head straight to the Royal Naval ship *Shoreham* stationed at Williamsburg, Virginia, and anxious to reunite with the *Whydah* and their booty, the men of the *Marianne* voted to sail away.

Upon landing on Block Island, the pirates released Captain Beer, who eventually reached his home in Newport, Rhode Island, on May 1, 1717.

Allowing Williams to visit his family while offloading their merchandise, the crew of the *Marianne* remained on a short time. Leisurely they cruised through the Long Island Sound, stopping at Gardiner Island to visit, as had William Kidd, before continuing their journey.

On the afternoon of Friday, April 26, 1717, the weather suddenly turned worse. The sky darkened, the winds began to blow harder, and the waves got dangerously high. Williams chose to find a safe shelter for the *Marianne* between Gardiner Island and eastern Long Island to wait out the coming storm. His decision saved their lives.

That same morning the pirates on the *Whydah* could not resist one more prize. The *Mary Anne*, a pink originally from Dublin, captained by Andrew Crumpstey, was carrying a full cargo of Madeira wine bound for New York Harbor. A pink is a ship with a narrow overhanging stern. They gave Captain Crumpstey one of their water-logged prize ships and took over the *Mary Anne*. Dispensing the wine throughout the ship, Bellamy ordered their course north by northwest, not toward Maine and Damariscove Island, but Cape Cod, specifically Eastham.

According to the survivors, Bellamy told his crew they were heading to Cape Cod to stock up on fresh food, water, and other provisions. The folklore of Eastham states his real reason was to reunite with Mary Hallett, proving to her father he was wealthy enough for her hand in marriage.

By three in the afternoon the fog was too thick to safely navigate the dangerous shoals of Cape Cod. Their luck held out when a local trading sloop, the *Fisher*, sailed toward them. Ascertaining that the captain, Robert Ingols, knew the coast well enough to navigate through any weather conditions, the pirates seized his ship and forced him onto the *Whydah* to guide them all safely through the fog.

By ten that evening the weather turned into one of the most violent nor'easter storms (a macroscale cyclone) the area could remember.

The pirates on the *Mary Anne* were too drunk to sail her properly and lost sight of the *Whydah*'s guiding lanterns. With thirty-foot waves crashing against the *Mary Anne*'s hull, men began to cut down her masts to lessen the strain on the ship's integrity. A crewman began to turn the great wheel, pointing the ship's bow toward shore. They hoped to prevent the ship from riding down the crest of a wave, crashing into the seabed, and splitting in two.

The *Ann Galley* also lost sight of the *Whydah*'s light but managed to stay close to the trading ship *Fisher*. Richard Nolan on the *Ann Galley* ordered the anchor dropped and yelled against the wind for the *Fisher* to do the same. Nolan hoped the iron anchors would be strong enough to secure both ships to the ocean floor, enabling them to ride out the storm. They now had no other options but to pray the anchors held tight while they fought against the churning waters a few hundred yards offshore.

Some miles north from the drama of the *Ann Galley*, the winds were blowing the *Whydah* straight toward the shore below the cliffs of Eastham. Bellamy also realized that, with the severe storm conditions, the only option they had was to drop both half-ton anchors and hope the anchors would hold. With the winds increasing past gale force and walls of water crashing over the main deck, the pirates felt the anchors begin to drag along the sea bottom. Their only hope for surviving the night was to bring the ship as gently as possible toward the shoreline.

Bellamy gave the order to cut the anchor ropes and turn the bow toward the beach. He hoped to give his men a chance of grabbing any bit of ship debris and making it to shore. To everyone's horror, the ship did not respond to the great wheel and turn, but remained on its deadly course. The winds pushed the *Whydah* backward, her stern first crashing the vessel against the jagged cliffs. Cannons broke loose and rolled across the deck, rigging crashed to the deck, and splintered wood shot across the deck like arrows. According to a survivor, "one pirate was thrown across the deck so hard his shoulder bone became completely embedded in the handle of a pewter teapot."

By Saturday morning the hull of the *Whydah* had broken in two, throwing the bodies of men, dead and alive, into the still-churning fast water. Out of some 165 men (including Captain Samuel Bellamy), only two managed to survive: John Julian, a Mosquito Indian from Cape Cod, and Thomas Davis, the carpenter who had pleaded with Bellamy to be set free.

Exhausted and fighting through the continuing rain, it took hours for Davis to reach Samuel Harding's farmhouse some two miles up the cliffs from the wreckage. Once Harding understood what Davis was saying, he had Davis guide him back to the wreck. Together they lashed all they could to Harding's horse, rescued John Julian, and, returned to the farmhouse.

While Davis and Julian recovered by the fire, Harding, his brother Abiah, and their neighbors Edward Knowles and Jonathan Cole returned to the wreck multiple times. They not only grabbed cargo, but stripped anything of value off corpses. By the time John Doane, the justice of the peace, arrived on the beach, there was nothing of value left to collect. Doane arrested the two pirates at Harding's house and sent them to the local gaol.

The *Mary Anne* and her crew survived the storm. Having sighted the wreck, John Cole and William Smith, two local men, rowed out in the driving rain and rescued the entire crew. They brought them all to Cole's home to recoup from their harrowing experience. All seemed well until Alexander Mackconachy, one of the pirate's captives, informed Cole that the men he was sheltering were pirates.

Fearing capture, the pirates ran from the house. Exhausted from fighting to keep their ship afloat all night, the men staggered to the Eastham Tavern, hoping to purchase horses for their escape. Fearing the pirates, Cole had alerted John Doane. He arrested them all, pirates and former captives, and temporarily locked them in the Barnstable gaol.

The pirates on the *Ann Galley* and *Fisher* had also survived the storm. They decided to load everything onto the *Ann Galley*, leaving the *Fisher* to drift unmanned, and head to the rendezvous point. On April 29 they landed on Monhegan Island, some ten miles off Maine. With fresh water and easy cod fishing, the pirates settled in and waited for the others to arrive. Unless they confused the two, why they did not continue the fifteen miles to Damariscove Island is anybody's guess. After weeks of waiting they gave up hope that anyone else had survived, and they sailed south to the Bahamas.

Paul Williams and the crew of the *Marianne* arrived at Damariscove Island on or about May 20, 1717. After waiting five days they realized no other men would be arriving. They set sail again on May 25, receiving the news of the *Whydah*'s fate from a passing Salem schooner. Knowing there was nothing to do but put as much distance as they could between themselves and the law, Williams sailed the *Marianne* for the Caribbean.

All the captured men from Bellamy's fleet were taken under heavy guard to Boston and thrown into the notorious iron cages inside the stone prison. Though the men were captured in May, they rotted in prison until October 18, 1717. During that time they specifically requested Reverend Cotton Mather be the clergyman to administer to them daily.

The eight surviving pirates from the pirate fleet were led to the courthouse in irons: Thomas Davis, 22 years, born in Wales; Simon Van Vorst, 24 years, born in New York; John Brown, 25 years, born in Jamaica; Thomas Baker, 29 years, born in Flushing, Holland; Hendrick Quintor, 25 years, born in Amsterdam; Peter Cornelius Hoff,

34 years, born in Sweden; John Sheean, 24 years, born in Nantes, France; and Thomas South, 30 years, born in Boston, England. All were brought to the admiralty court on charges of piracy in seizing the "free trading Vessel or Pink called the *Mary Anne*." John Julian was not among the tried men. It is not known whether he died in prison or, because he was a Mosquito Indian, was taken to the slave blocks.

Samuel Shute, captain-governor of the provinces of Massachusetts and New Hampshire, officiated as president of the court. The court members were William Dummer, lieutenant governor; John Menzies, judge of the vice-admiralty; John Jekyll, collector of plantation duties; and Captain Thomas Smart, commander of the HMS *Squirrel*. Also in attendance were the men who sat on the council: Elisha Hutchinson, Penn Townsend, Andrew Belcher, John Cushing, Nathaniel Norden, John Wheelwright, Benjamin Lynde, Thomas Hutchinson, and Thomas Fitch.

Thomas Davis and Thomas South were able to prove their innocence and were acquitted. The other men were found guilty of the charges. On Friday, November 15, 1717, the former pirates were hanged "at Charlestown Ferry within the flux and reflux of the Sea."

Stretching for miles across the seafloor, buried under ten to thirty feet of shifting sand in murky water, the *Whydah* remained untouched for 267 years. In 1984 treasure hunter Barry Clifford discovered her wreck in twenty feet of water off the coast of Cape Cod. The enormous amount of treasure Clifford has so far recovered is estimated in the hundreds of millions of dollars.

Along with Samuel Bellamy's immense treasure, two items of special note were recovered: a skeletal right leg bone (fibula) and a foot encased in a woven French silk stocking no more than two inches wide with an expensive leather heeled shoe with a silver buckle enclosure. After extensive laboratory testing, it was confirmed the fibula belonged to a boy between the ages of eight and eleven.

And what of the love story that ended so tragically? Did Mary Hallett truly exist?

Mr. Ken Kinkor of the Expedition Whydah Museum in Provincetown, Massachusetts, discovered that the romantic folklore of Samuel Bellamy and Mary Hallett might contain a kernel of truth. By going through church records, Mr. Kinkor verified there indeed lived a Mary Hallett in Eastham, Cape Cod. According to her birth records Mary was 21 years old in the year 1715. She was the daughter of John Hallett, who had immigrated from Yarmouth, England. Mr. Hallett had become one of the wealthiest settlers in the Eastham area.

Mary's eldest brother, John Jr., married a local girl, Mehitable Brown, whose family owned the Great Island Tavern. The tavern, situated in Billingsgate, catered to mariners. Mary, being the sixth child of ten in the family, could have been living with her brother and working at the tavern. Mary Hallett could have indeed met Samuel Bellamy.

She died in April 1751, unwed and childless.

CHAPTER ELEVEN

George Lowther, John Massey, and Charles Harris

WITH SO MANY SHIPS BEING SEIZED BY PIRATES IN THE 1720S, IT IS no wonder it became inevitable for many captured men to become pirates themselves, and therefore have their lives forever interwoven with the trade.

George Lowther walked along the docks of London in 1721, looking for employment. Though he was an inexperienced seaman, he signed onto the *Gambia Castle*, as second mate to Captain Charles Russel. The ship belonged to the Royal African Company, whose main source of income was the selling of African captives as slaves to the Caribbean Islands and North American colonies. The ship was scheduled to sail to St. James Island, Gambia, Africa (now known as Kunta Kinteh Island) and dock at the Royal African Company trading settlement, the military garrison, and castle.

Previously, pirates had stormed St. James Island, disarmed all the soldiers at the fort, stripped the castle, and looted the merchants and traders of everything of value. Additionally, they raided the castle's treasure room, which was filled with gold ingots and ivory.

The ship's additional passengers for this particular voyage were soldiers under the command of Captain John Massey. The captain's order was simple: to protect the settlement from any further pirate attacks. Captain Massey was personally guaranteed that he and his men would be provided with comfortable accommodations and ample provisions from the citizens and merchants on the island.

When the *Gambia Castle* arrived on the island in May of 1721, the conditions on land were deplorable. None of the terms promised to the seamen or soldiers were fulfilled. Even the newly appointed governor of the island, Colonel Whitney, who happened to arrive the very same day with his son, considered returning to England as soon as possible once he stepped foot on the island.

With no accommodations available on land as promised, the men of the *Gambia Castle* were forced to spend months aboard ship. Captain Russel staunchly refused to listen to any of the seamen's complaints or suggestions. Captain Massey saw the brewing tension among all the men. He tried to convince Governor Whitney to remedy the situation between the seamen, soldiers, and the island's tradesmen before out-and-out mutiny became imminent. Neither the governor nor Captain Russel would listen to reason.

George Lowther had voiced his concerns repeatedly. When Lowther approached Captain Russel once more concerning the conditions onboard ship, Russel ordered him flogged for insubordination. The ship's crew refused to let the order be carried out.

Fearing for his life at the hands of Russel, Lowther, with the backing of his crewmates, locked the captain in his cabin. Lowther sent a desperate note to Massey for help. Seeing no other way out of their current situation, Captain Massey approached his soldiers with a proposition. They could remain on the island or all decide to leave on the *Gambia Castle* and return to England.

Agreeing to the latter suggestion, the soldiers raided all the fort's provisions, along with eleven pipes of brandy from the governor's private cellar. (A pipe is a specific size of wooden cask, the capacity of which is equivalent to 126 US gallons or 476.96 UK liters.) Captain Massey ordered the cannons they had brought to the fort be dismantled and mounted onto the ship's deck. With the armed soldiers aboard, the men forced Captain Russel off his vessel. The men all voted George Lowther captain, and the *Gambia Castle* set sail for England.

Once at sea Lowther realized how their actions would appear before the owners of the Royal African Company. The company's majority shareholders consisted of government officials, personal friends of the king, and other lords of the realm. Lowther knew the shareholders would demonstrate little sympathy with regards to the men and the deplorable living conditions they had to endure on St. James, which had prompted their actions—their only concern was profits.

Gathering the men on deck, Lowther explained the situation as he saw it. Simply put, no matter what the reason had been for leaving the island and marooning Captain Russel, they would all be considered mutineers. If they returned to England, it surely meant imprisonment or death. Lowther believed the only option left was for them to take their chances and turn pirate. If any man did not wish to participate in the endeavor, he would be safely set ashore somewhere to do as he pleased. All fifty soldiers and seamen agreed to go on the account. Lowther drew up ship's articles (one of the only such documents to have survived all these years). Changing the ship's name to *Happy Delivery*, they set sail for the West Indies.

Putting on all sails, the ship reached Barbados in the Caribbean on June 20 and began seizing any vessel it encountered. At this time in his pirating career, Lowther rarely fired at potential prey; his favorite tactic became ramming his intended target until the ship surrendered.

Off the island of Hispaniola, the *Happy Delivery* spotted a French sloop. Massey convinced Lowther to attempt a different tactic. The pirates raised the French flag on their main mast and came alongside the sloop. Pretending to be a merchant, Massey boarded their prey. Upon being introduced to the captain, he produced a flintlock pistol and ordered the Frenchman to have his crew transfer their entire cargo. Thirty pipes of brandy, bolts of Chintz cloth, and five hogsheads of wine along with £70 ($35,000) in coins were moved to the *Happy Delivery*. (A hogshead is a specific size of wooden cask, the capacity of which is equivalent to 63 US gallons or 238.48 UK liters.) When the pirates were ready to depart, Captain Massey handed the French captain £5 ($2,500) of his own coins for being such a gracious host to him.

The life of a pirate, however, was not to Massey's liking. He was a soldier at heart, not a pirate. When they captured another sloop, Massey and ten of his soldiers chose to sail the sloop to Jamaica and state their case, against Lowther's dire warnings.

Parting ways with Massey, Lowther sailed toward Puerto Rico, where he captured a two-ship fleet. Ironically, the fleet turned out to be a Spanish pirate ship holding captive a Bristol merchant ship. Instead of the friendly encounter usually conducted at sea between two pirates, Lowther, having no love for the Spanish, seized and ransacked both vessels. He set the Spaniards adrift in one of their own longboats, took all the Englishmen captives, and torched both vessels.

Needing to careen their ship, the pirates sailed for a secluded island. In the warm waters of the Caribbean, every six weeks to three months the wooden-hulled ships needed to be cleaned of barnacles, Teredo worms, and seaweed to guarantee they could maneuver properly. There the men remained, repairing their vessel and carousing with the natives, until the end of December 1721. Determined to seize as many ships as possible, the crew of the *Happy Delivery* set sail for Honduras in Central America. Desperate for fresh water and provisions, they detoured first to Grand Cayman Island (between Cuba and Jamaica).

It was here that George Lowther met the pirate Edward "Ned" Low (a.k.a Loe or Lowe). Low's ship, with only a pirate crew of thirteen, was in such poor condition that it could not sail far distances. Lowther offered them the opportunity to join the *Happy Delivery*. Agreeing, Ned Low became Lowther's lieutenant and the crews merged into one.

Captain George Lowther and his company at Port Mayo in the Gulph (Gulf) of Matique.
CREDIT: UNKNOWN, C. 1734

By then news of Lowther's exploits had reached England, and the hunt for him was on. A rumor that the HMS *Feversham* had captured Lowther in Barbados had Captain Charles Russel sail from Plymouth, Massachusetts, to Barbados to confront his former second-in-command and retrieve his ship. Unfortunately for Russel, the rumor proved false.

Ignorant of these facts, Lowther and crew continued to sail along the coast of Honduras. They captured a newly built sloop sailing from Rhode Island. Since the ship was in excellent condition, Lowther chose to retain the vessel and start a pirate fleet of his own. He mounted eight deck guns and ten swivel guns on his new prize, the *Ranger*, and handed the captaincy to Ned Low.

Back in Boston, 24-year-old Charles Harris signed onto the *Greyhound* as her first mate and navigator. The ship was a merchantman that hauled prized logwood from the jungles of Honduras. On January 10, 1722, with the *Greyhound* loaded to capacity with logwood, the ship began its return to Boston.

Earlier in the day the lookout on the *Greyhound* had spotted a ship but no one took any great notice until the afternoon, when the watch noticed the ship change its course to intercept the *Greyhound*.

The *Greyhound*'s captain, Benjamin Edwards, decided to prepare for the worst and called all hands on deck. When the other ship came into close proximity, it ran up a pirate black flag emblazoned with a white skeleton—the pursuing ship was Lowther's *Happy Delivery*. Without waiting for a response, Lowther ordered a broadside. Captain Edwards, unwilling to yield, ordered his men to return fire. The gun battle raged for over an hour, until Captain Edwards realized the pirate ship had more guns and ammunition. He'd heard the stories of pirate tortures if resistance to them proved too great. Fearing for the lives of his crew, Edwards decided to surrender the battle he knew he couldn't win.

The pirates swarmed over the ship's railing only to discover the ship's cargo was logwood. They went berserk. Since both Lowther and Low were sadistic individuals, they did not prevent their men from torturing the crew of the *Greyhound*. Lowther and Low even participated in the atrocities. Once their rage dissipated, the pirates ordered Captain Edwards and his crew into the *Greyhound*'s longboats and rowed them to the *Happy Delivery*, torching the *Greyhound*.

Even though they had previously tortured the men, once aboard the *Happy Delivery*, the pirates handed each one a tankard of rum and an invitation to join their crew. When Captain Edwards and his crew refused, the pirates permitted most of them to board the next ship seized and sail back to Boston.

Charles Harris, being a navigator, was forced to remain aboard the pirate ship along with five others from the *Greyhound* crew: Christopher Atwell, Henry Smith, Joseph Willis, David Lindsay, and Francis Farrington Spriggs. Days later the pirates finally persuaded the men to sign the ship's articles. When Lowther captured a sloop out of Jamaica, he handed the captaincy of the sloop to Harris.

For the next fourteen months the three pirate ships terrorized the seas until the fierce personality clashes between George Lowther and Ned Low finally came to a head. Instead of starting a bloodbath aboard the fleet, the men voted to split company. On May 28, 1722, Lowther and forty-four men on *Happy Delivery* sailed toward New England. Low sailed the *Ranger* with forty-five men toward the West Indies. Harris's crew voted to join Ned Low.

Having earlier departed from the pirate fleet, Captain Massey and his soldiers sailed directly to Jamaica. The soldiers quickly dispersed throughout the island's citizenry. However, John Massey chose to present his case in its entirety directly to Governor Nicholas Lawes, insisting he had acted the way he had to save lives: "twas to save so many of his Majesty's Subject from perishing, and that his Design was to return to England; but Lowther conspiring with the greater part of the Company, went a pyrating with the Ship; and that he had taken this Opportunity to leave him, and surrender himself and Vessel to his Excellency."

Governor Lawes listened to Massey's entire narrative and, noting he had not killed a person, saw no real harm done. The governor promised Massey his favored opinion. Massey even joined Governor Lawes on the sloop *Happy*, when he mounted a search for George Lowther. After receiving the governor's certificate of pardon, along with a large sum of money, Massey returned to England.

After he arrived in London, Captain Massey did a bizarre thing. Not trying to escape notice, he wrote to the deputy governor and directors of the Royal African Company, explaining all the circumstances and all of his deeds. His letter revealed some interesting traits about the man himself. He admitted he went pirating with Lowther yet added this, speaking of himself in the third person:

> . . . but excuses it as Rashness and Inadvertency in himself, occasioned by his being ill used, contrary to the Promises that had been made him, and the Expectations he had entertained; but own'd, that he deserved to die for what he had done; yet, if they had Generosity enough to forgive him, as he was still capable to do them Service, as a Soldier, so he should be ready to do it; but if they resolved to prosecute him, he begg'd only this Favour, that he might not be hang'd like a Dog, but die like a Soldier, as he had been bred from his Childhood, that is, that he might be shot.

Their response: "He could not be forgiven but should be fairly hang'd." Captain John Massey surrendered himself to the Old Bailey. Not considered a flight risk, he paid a £100 ($50,000) bail and was released. Massey's trial began on July 5, 1723. Captain Charles Russel, as well as Governor Whitney's son, traveling from St. James Island, testified against him. He was convicted of mutiny and piracy upon the high seas. On July 26, 1723, at Tyburn, London, on Execution Dock, Captain Massey was not dealt the death of his request. He was not shot with the respect given to a soldier, but hanged.

Sailing alone once again after the fleet breakup on May 28, 1722, the crew of the *Happy Delivery* proceeded to successfully capture ships on the mid-Atlantic. They sacked a number of fishing boats off of New York, which yielded little treasure or provisions.

Captain Lowther's luck changed on June 3 when the ship *Mary Galley* sailed into view, homeward bound from Barbados to Boston. Fearing for the lives of his civilian passengers, Captain Peter King chose not to resist the pirates. The treasure haul was impressive. They secured fourteen hogsheads of alcohol along with an additional full barrel of rum. (A barrel of rum has the fluid capacity of 43 US gallons and 164 UK liters.) In addition to the liquor, the pirates removed six barrels of loose sugar, several casks of sugar loaves and cases of pepper, and six black slaves. All the passengers were robbed of their valuable possessions, money, and plates. (Passengers and crews needed to provide their own dinnerware and utensils on a voyage.) After the pirates finished ransacking the ship, they let the *Mary Galley* proceed with all crew and passengers unharmed. When the ship arrived at Boston Harbor on June 14, the story of her seizure made all the newspapers and broadsheets.

Lowther took to sailing along the capes of the Chesapeake, never ceasing to hunt for ships. Due to his frequent and successful attacks, trade along the route had stopped entirely. Benjamin Franklin's newspaper, the *New England Courant*, made the very satirical note "that for some time no man-of-war has been seen in the vicinity, who by dear experience, we know, love Trading better than Fighting."

Lowther and his crew aroused such fear of pirates that every vessel sighted at sea was presumed to be sailing under a black flag. Rumors of the *Happy Delivery* attacking all up and down the Atlantic coast permeated the public. By the spring of 1723, when he was supposedly attacking New England, Lowther had instead followed the weather patterns and steered for Newfoundland.

With their provisions dangerously low, the pirates' luck held out. They captured Captain John Hood's schooner, the *Swift*. The ship was full of provisions; the pirates took all they needed, forced three men to join their crew, and then let the ship resume its journey. Now sailing toward the West Indies, the pirates continued to plunder and force additional men to join them.

By October 1723 Lowther knew the ship was in desperate need of careening. The pirates sailed to the desolate island of Blanco (Blanquilla) off the northeast coast of Venezuela and anchored at a small cove on the northwest end. The six-mile-wide island was heavily wooded, with thick underbrush and smooth, low-lying beaches. Inhabited only by ample numbers of sea turtles and iguana along with a steady supply of fresh water, the island was the perfect place to refit the ship. The pirates began the laborious task of removing all the guns from the deck, taking down sails and rigging, and removing everything they could physically walk off the ship.

Waiting for high tide so they could more easily haul the lighter ship onto the beach, a lookout spotted a boat on the horizon. The sloop *Eagle*, commanded by Captain Walter Moore and owned by Colonel Otley, a shareholder of the South-Sea Company, was heading for Cumana, Venezuela. Since the island of Blanco was not a common trade route destination, Captain Moore grew suspicious of the *Happy Delivery*.

Captain Moore fired a signal shot for the men to show their colors. The pirates hoisted the flag of St. George on their topmast. Instinctively knowing this was no trading ship, Moore ordered the *Eagle* closer to investigate. Panicked, the pirates already ashore fired their cannons at the approaching ship. Those pirates still remaining aboard cut the anchor cable and ordered those on the beach to pull the ship to land for cover. A gun battle ensued until the pirates realized they were outgunned and trapped. Those on the beach ran into the woods. Lowther and twelve others who were trapped aboard ship escaped out of the captain's cabin window.

Captain Moore first secured the *Happy Delivery* as his prize, managing to get her afloat. Then he personally led a shore party with twenty-five of his men to search for the pirates. After five days of combing the island, they captured a number of pirates, but George Lowther was not among them.

Deciding to search no longer, Captain Moore sailed to St. Christopher Island (now known as St. Kitts) with his prisoners and prize ship. The Spanish governor, so pleased with Moore's actions, turned the *Happy Delivery* over to him and his crew of thirty-five to sell and split the profits. The governor also ordered a sloop of twenty-three soldiers to return to the island of Blanco and capture the remaining pirates. The search party found four more pirates, whom the governor condemned to a life of slavery as rowers in the bowels of Spanish galley ships.

A few soldiers emerging from the deep brush insisted they had discovered the body of George Lowther with a bullet through his head from an apparent suicide, a flintlock pistol at his side. Nothing was mentioned of the other three pirates and a young boy supposedly still hiding on the island.

A vice-admiralty court was called into session on March 11, 1724. The following men were charged with and convicted of piracy: John Churchill, Edward Mackdonald, Nicholas Lewis, Richard West, Samuel Levercott, Robert White, John Shaw, Andrew Hunter, Jonathan Delve, Matthew Freebarn, and Henry Watson. Three other men, Ralph Cando, Roger Grange, and Robert Willis, were acquitted.

On March 20, 1724, gallows were erected between the high and low watermark, as required by admiralty law. The eleven condemned pirates were hanged.

News of Lowther's suicide spread throughout the Caribbean Islands and Atlantic coast. Ship owners and captains heaved a sigh of relief that one more pirate had perished. Since George Lowther was heard of no more, he was surely dead. However, the soldiers claiming to have found him did not produce Lowther's body for identification.

Did Lowther commit suicide like they claimed? Glory and monetary compensation typically accompanied physical proof of an infamous pirate's death. Knowing a cash reward would be their due, why didn't the ship's officers or Captain Moore himself retrieve the body as proof of Lowther's demise? There was no logical reason for the other pirates on the island to kill him; perhaps Lowther died of natural causes. No one knows for sure. What is known is that during his seventeen-month pirate spree, George Lowther captured thirty-seven ships.

Charles Harris, as captain of the captured Jamaican sloop, was still sailing with Ned Low and his former mate from the *Gambia Castle*, Francis Farrington Spriggs, along the New England coast, capturing whatever boats they encountered on their way to Nova Scotia. Soon they arrived at Port Roseway, Nova Scotia (now known as Shelburne). There the pirates captured a pink, the *Mary*, from Captain Joseph Dolliber. Low decided to use the *Mary* as his personal flagship. He renamed the ship *Fancy* and turned the captaincy of the *Ranger* over to Harris.

Port Roseway being a small fishing village, the pirates knew that many fishing vessels from Marblehead, Massachusetts, would seek safe anchorage at her harbor during the evening before sailing out again in the morning. Harris and Low captured and looted thirteen such ships in rapid succession for provisions, water, coin, and men. Again Low preferred one of the fishing vessels, so he gave the captaincy of the *Fancy* to Spriggs. Low personally took command of the captured ship the *Fortune*.

While Low and Spriggs continued to terrorize the Atlantic coast and West Indies, there is no mention of Charles Harris from December 1722 until May 23, 1723. It was on that day in May, off the coast of South Carolina, that Harris was spotted in command of forty-eight men on the eight-gun mounted *Ranger*. Sailing with Ned Low, who boasted seventy men on the ten-gun mounted *Fortune*, the pirates were heading toward New England. As newspapers printed accounts of a pirate fleet capturing ships and torturing crewmembers, the colonists rallied and demanded greater provincial government action.

The man-of-war HMS *Greyhound* (ironically not the same ship that Harris and Spriggs had originally crewed), commanded by Captain Peter Solgard, steered off course and went in search of pirates. Built a mere three years earlier, the *Greyhound* was mounted with twenty guns and carried a crew of 130 men.

On June 10, 1723, at four thirty in the morning, while sailing the Atlantic near Long Island, New York, the *Greyhound*'s lookout noticed two ships, as specks on the horizon, sailing in close formation. Assuming they were Harris and Low, Solgard made sure the pirates spotted his ship from a far distance. He deliberately ordered the *Greyhound* to reverse course as if it were fleeing the oncoming ships. If the two vessels gave chase, Solgard would know they were pirates. As he suspected, the ships altered course and sailed toward the man-of-war. The distance between them gave Captain Solgard time to prepare for the fight he knew would come.

Thinking they were chasing a whaler, by eight o'clock both pirate ships closed in. Hoisting black flags, they each fired a gun at the fleeing ship. Still some three quarters of a mile from the *Greyhound*, the pirates realized their target was trying to outrun them. Harris and Low ordered their black flags lowered to be replaced by solid red ones. A pirate's red flag signified "no quarter given." It meant if the prey did not surrender immediately, death would be their fate.

Captain Solgard had his men hold their fire until the *Greyhound* maneuvered abreast of the two ships. Solgard then ordered his larboard (left side, now known as port) and starboard (right side, still called starboard) guns to fire round shot (cannonballs) and grapeshot at the two ships. Grapeshot is a number of small cannonballs secured in a cloth bag that scatters the balls when fired forward, similar to buckshot. For two hours the gun battle inflicted severe damage to all three vessels.

Firing a shot during a gun battle was not a fast or easy one-man operation. Ideally five men manned a single gun. After unlashing the gun carriage from the railing, the men would pull the weapon backward with ropes, leaving no more than eighteen inches of space between the gun's muzzle and the gunwale (inside wall under the railing). One man would open and secure the gun port, the hinged square wooden flap on the outside of a ship. The flap was lifted open from the outside by a rope pulled over the rail and tied to an inner rail ring, exposing the open hole.

While this was being done, the other members of the gun crew prepared their tools, which were numerous. The most important ones were a wooden bucket filled with seawater and another one filled with sand placed on either side of the gun carriage. Along with the buckets, the rammer or ramrod, swabbing sponge, wormer, and linstock were readied. The wormer, a double spiral metal point similar to intertwined corkscrews attached to a wooden rod, cleaned out the gun of any residue wadding after a battle. If the gun misfired, which happened, the wormer was used to carefully dislodge the shot and wadding with skill, without sparking an explosion. The swabbing sponge, a wooden cylinder the diameter of the gun bore, covered with lambskin or a bristle brush, was mounted on a long wooden staff. Often it would be mounted on the opposite end of the rammer. The rammer was the same diameter as the gun bore. These were placed into one of the two barrels to prevent them from rolling around the deck.

Waiting for a powder monkey to bring up the loaded paper cartridges from the powder room below, the gun captain would light a "slow match," attaching it to create the linstock. The slow match was a loosely woven piece of long coiled hemp cord previously boiled in a mixture of saltpeter and dried. It was then attached and looped via a hook to a wooden staff approximately three feet in length. If the linstock was set aside during a battle, it was propped up in either the sand or a water bucket, to prevent accidental fires aboard ships.

This guaranteed the ash from the slow match fell onto a safe surface and not the wooden deck.

The gun loader cleaned the touchhole vent on the top of the gun and the grooved area, called the base ring, of any damp or clumped gunpowder with a pick, also called a priming iron. Approximately nine inches in length, the pick resembled a thick sewing needle: sharp at one end, blunt at the other, with a loop large enough to hook a finger through.

A paper powder cartridge, measured with the correct amount of gunpowder for that specific gun, was then loaded, secured in place by wadding (either cloth or paper), and seated (pushed carefully) with the dry ramrod. Next the shot was loaded; another bit of wading could be used to secure the lead shot and seated. The loader had to make sure the shot did not come out and roll across the deck while he was moving or angling the gun. If not loaded properly, a gun could misfire. In the chaos of battle a gun could be loaded wrong or double loaded. To prevent a catastrophe from happening, the loader would have marked the ramrod handle, designating the space depths after each component was loaded.

With brute force and side tackle ropes, the men "ran out" the gun, rolling the gun carriage toward the gunwale with the muzzle protruding above water. Positioned to the desired angle with the help of handspikes, the gun was ready to be fired. The loader pushed the pick through the touchhole, opening the paper gunpowder cartridge seated in the back and pouring gunpowder into the touchhole until the powder was level with the base ring. With the command of "fire in the hole," the gun captain and crew moved to the side of the carriage for safety. The gun captain ignited the gunpowder cartridge.

The gunner lowered the slow match to the base ring. He never directly ignited the powder over the touchhole. The air that escaped with the flame that was created, called the huff, would extinguish the slow match. Once fired, the entire gun carriage would recoil. It was not uncommon for a gun to jump its secure ropes, break free, and roll across a deck, crushing or pinning men down.

The sponger, the pirate who cleaned and cooled the gun, would quickly take the wet swabbing sponge rod and swab (wash) out the hot bore until water or air bubbles came out of the touchhole. With the gun cleaned and cooled to prevent exploding sparks during the reload, the sponger stepped aside. The process was then repeated. A very well-trained gun crew took two to five minutes to load, aim correctly, and fire. In the heat of battle, with several guns firing in succession, a veil of white smoke would hang over a ship's deck.

A sure hit during a gun battle could inflict crippling damage to men and ship. Men were in constant danger from falling rigging, tackle, sails, flying pieces of splintered wood, a slippery blood-drenched deck, and rolling guns.

Another dangerous element in a gun battle was the unpredictability of the wind. Changing wind direction or velocity was a constant major factor in the success or failure of an encounter.

When the wind suddenly slackened, and with the tide of the fighting going against them, Charles Harris and Ned Low both ordered their men to take to the ship's oars and row away from the engagement. Eighty-six of the *Greyhound*'s crew followed suit, taking to their own oars in pursuit.

At two thirty in the afternoon, the three ships caught up with each other. Within firing range the gun barrage resumed. Captain Solgard managed to separate the *Fortune* and *Ranger*. At four o'clock a lucky shot from the *Greyhound* brought down the mainsail of the *Ranger*.

Captain Harris looked on in horror as he watched the *Fortune* tack about and change course. Instead of closing in to attack the *Greyhound* and helping Harris to a possible victory, Captain Low cowardly fled the battle. Realizing their situation now to be hopeless, Harris and his crew surrendered. By five o'clock the crew of the *Ranger* was clamped in irons aboard the *Greyhound*.

Familiar with Low's regular haunts, Captain Solgard had Harris on the *Greyhound*'s quarterdeck, assisting in chasing him down. They lost sight of the *Fortune* at approximately eight o'clock near Block Island, between Long Island and Rhode Island. Harris suggested Low would likely head for Boston.

The *Boston News-Letter* and Benjamin Franklin's *New England Courant* ran similar accounts of the chase, battle, and capture of the *Ranger*. They also mentioned that Joseph Sweetser of Charlestown, Massachusetts, and Charles Harris had been listed in previous editions of the newspapers as being forced men.

On June 12 Captain Solgard, with his prisoners off-loaded, refitted the ship and set out in pursuit of Captain Low.

The *New England Courant* issued on June 24, 1723, listed "An Account of the Names, Ages, and places of Birth these Men taken by his Majesty's Ship Greyhound, in the Pirate Sloop called the Ranger, and now confined in his Majesty's Gaol in Rhode Island."

The thirty-seven men and boys captured off the *Ranger* did not languish in the gaol for long. One of them—Thomas Reeve, 30 years old, hailing from the County of Rutland, England—died before the trial dates became public. For the others, the trials began on Wednesday morning, July 10, 1723, in Newport, Rhode Island. They continued for three days. The following men presided over the Court of Admiralty: William Dummer, lieutenant governor of Massachusetts; John Valentine, advocate-general; Samuel Cranston, governor of Rhode Island; John Menzies, judge of the admiralty; John Lechmere, surveyor-general; Richard Ward, register; Jahleel Brinton, provost-marshal; and Nathaniel Pain, Addington Davenport, Thomas Fitch, and Spencer Phipps.

The accused men were brought to trial in groups. They all pleaded not guilty. Unfortunately for the pirates, many survivors who had been seized by their pirate fleet willingly appeared before the court to testify as eyewitnesses to their crimes.

Though many of the men began as legitimately forced men, the court issued a pronouncement: Once a man willingly took even a single coin from the illegal act of piracy, then he, in the eyes of the court, had turned pirate. Eight individuals were deemed innocent and released:

Henry Barnes, age 22, Island of Barbados. Proof was forced, took no coin.

Thomas Child, age 15, Edinburgh. Forced onto *Ranger* four days before capture.

John Fletcher, age 17, Edinburgh. Forced musician, played violin. Took no coin.

John Hincher (Hinchard), age 27, Edinburgh. Forced doctor. Took no coin.

Thomas Jones, age 17, Flur, Wales. Proof he was forced, took no coin.

Thomas Mumper (Umper), age 21, Martha's Vineyard. A servant, took no coin.

Joseph Sweetser (Switzer), age 24, Boston. Proof he was forced.

John Wilson, age 23, New London County, Connecticut. Proof he was forced.

Two men—John Brown, age 17, and Patrick Cunningham, age 25, both from Liverpool, England—were declared guilty but received a one-year reprieve, after which they were required to enter the king's military service.

By the evening of July 12, all twenty-six men on trial for piracy were sentenced to death by hanging. Their names were called out:

Charles Harris, age 25, London. Captain.

William Blads (Blades), age 28, Rhode Island.

John Bright, age 25, Westminster, England.

James Brinkly, age 28, Suffolk, England.

John Brown, age 29, County Durham, England.

Charles Church, age 21, St. Margaret's, Westminster, England.

Edward Eaton, age 38, Wrexham, Wales.

John Fitzgerald, age 21, Limerick, Ireland.

Thomas Hazel, age 50, Westminster, England.

Thomas Huggit, age 30, London, England.

Daniel Hyde (Hide), age 23, Virginia.

William Jones, age 28, London, England.

Peter Kneeves (Kewes), age 32, Exeter, Devon, England.

Abraham Lacy, age 21, Devonshire, England.

Edward Lawson, age 20, Isle of Man, England.

Francis Leyton (Layton), age 39, New York.

Joseph Libbey, age 21, Marblehead, Massachusetts.

Thomas Linister (Linisker), age 21, Lancashire, England.

Stephen Mundon, age 20, London, England.

Thomas Powel Jr. age 21, Wethersfield, Connecticut.

William Read, age 35, Londonderry, Ireland.

Owen Rice, age 27, South Wales.

Joseph Sawrd (Sound), age 28, Westminster, England.

William Shutfield, age 40, Lancaster, England.

John Tompkins, age 23, Gloucestershire, England.

John Waters (Walters), age 35, Devonshire, England. Quartermaster.

Waiting for their execution day, the pirates were visited daily by the clergy. They helped the men write letters to family and attempted to administer to their wretched souls.

On July 19, 1723, the convicted pirates were taken from the Newport gaol and paraded through the streets of Newport to the gallows constructed between the high and low watermark at Gravelly Point. This would become the largest number of pirates hanged at one time.

The popular method of public hanging was the short drop. The condemned would be standing on some form of stool, barrel, or small platform on the scaffold with the noose tight around his neck. The platform would be removed, leaving the condemned dangling mere inches off solid ground. This did not break his neck. As the man thrashed about with the instinct to breathe, his body weight pulled the noose tighter against his larynx as it slowly crushed his windpipe. It was a slow, agonizing death, taking fifteen to twenty minutes before finally asphyxiating the man.

The executions took place between noon and one o'clock in the afternoon. The townsfolk made a festive day of the hanging. Many picnicked on the grounds surrounding the scaffold or boated, all there to watch the spectacle.

As was the custom, each condemned man was allowed to address the crowd. Most said prayers to save their souls. Any and all statements given at gallows' edge were published in the papers and broadsheets along with an observational clerical treatise on the event.

The night before his execution, John Brown wrote a cautionary statement to the young in the crowd. He insisted that he had never truly turned pirate: "It was with the greatest Reluctancy and Horror of Mind and Conscience, I was compelled to go with them . . . and I can say my Heart and Mind never joined in those horrid Robberies, Conflagarations and Cruelties committed."

That same night, John Fitzgerald composed his death poem. After his execution it was printed and widely circulated:

> To mortal Men that daily live in Wickedness and Sin;
> This dying Counsel I do give, hoping you will begin
> To serve the Lord in Time of Youth his Precepts for to keep;
> To serve him so in Spirit and Truth, that you may mercy reap.
>
> ***
>
> In Youthful blooming Years was I, when I that Practice took;
> Of perpetrating Piracy, for filthy gain did look.
> To Wickedness as all were bent, our Lusts for to fulfill;
> To rob at Sea was our Intent, and perpetrate all Ill.
>
> ***
>
> I pray the Lord preserve you all and keep you from this End;
> O let Fitz-Gerald's great downfall unto your welfare tend.
> I to the Lord my soul bequeath, accept thereof I pray,
> My body to the Earth bequeath, dear Friends, adieu for aye.

The bodies were not tarred and gibbetted, as was the common custom. The remains of pirate Captain Charles Harris and crewmates lie in a mass unmarked grave between the high and low watermarks on Goat Island, situated off Newport, Rhode Island, in Narragansett Bay.

Chapter Twelve

Edward "Ned" Low and Francis Farrington Spriggs

THE PIRATE EDWARD "NED" LOW (A.K.A LOWE OR LOE) WAS A SADIS-
tic psychopath who reveled in torture and cannibalism. He was a true
stereotype of the barbaric pirate often portrayed in movies and novels.

Born in Westminster, England, to a family of illiterate thieves and
pickpockets, he began his bullying ways at a young age. He fought the
other boys living on the streets, taking their meager coins daily. The
others soon learned that to prevent a brutal beating from Ned Low,
they needed to just hand him what they had in their pockets.

As a teen he hung out with the carriage footmen employed by the
members of the House of Lords, playing "the whole game." The object
of the card game was to see how well you could cheat before getting
caught. Low would fight anyone who disputed any of his claims.

Not all of his family worked the wrong side of the law. One of his
older brothers convinced Low to join him working on a merchantman. Low sailed for four years until he decided to leave his life at sea
and remain in Boston, where he took a position as a ship-rigger at a
rigging house for eight years.

He fell in love and married Eliza Marble on August 12, 1714, in
the First Church of Boston (a Congregational and later Unitarian

Universalist church), Reverend Benjamin Wadsworth officiating. They had a son who died in infancy. In 1719 Eliza gave birth to their daughter, Elizabeth. A short time later, Eliza died. This seemed to tip Ned Low over the edge. He grew argumentative with his employer and quit his position. Unable to cope with the death of his wife, Low brought Elizabeth to Eliza's parents' house to be raised properly.

He signed onto a logwood sloop bound for the Bay of Honduras. A valuable and highly profitable purple dye was extracted from the wood of this particular tree. Once the ship had landed at the illegal logging camp, he was appointed patron of the boat. It was the prestigious position of foreman, overseeing the loading of wood from the jungle to the longboat and onto the sloop. Since they were essentially stealing the precious wood from a Spanish territory, his twelve-man crew was heavily armed at all times with muskets, flintlocks, and knives.

After one particular day of loading wood onto the sloop, the men were ready for their evening meal. The sloop's captain, however, insisted they return to shore and obtain one more load of logwood before they could retire for the night and eat. The captain, in his arrogance, attempted to appease the crew's agitation over his order by giving them a bottle of rum and suggesting that drinking it would make the loading go faster.

Enraged, Low grabbed one of the loaded muskets and fired at him, only to miss the captain but kill another man. Low and his men quickly rowed away from the sloop. With all their weapons on their boat, and resentful of the man's insult, the men all agreed to turn pirate. They voted Low their captain.

Leaving the area at daybreak, they set sail for the Cayman Islands. On the way they captured a small fishing vessel and stole it. It was at Grand Cayman Island that George Lowther and Ned Low met for the first time. Low and his men signed on with Lowther on his ship, the *Happy Delivery*. After they captured enough vessels to amass a fleet, Lowther handed Low his own command, the *Ranger*.

Having personalities too strong to work together without violence erupting throughout the entire pirate fleet, Low and Lowther parted ways on May 28, 1722. Low and forty-five men on the *Ranger*—including Charles Harris and Francis Farrington Spriggs, both formerly forced captives—immediately drew up ship's articles, signed their names, and set out searching for prey.

One of Low's first captures happened off Block Island when the *Ranger* seized a sloop under the command of James Cahoon. Brandishing cutlasses and flintlocks, the pirates took all the provisions, water, and ship's mainsail for their own ship. Before allowing the sloop to sail away, Low's men cut the ship's bowsprit sail and threw the rigging in the water. They hoped to prevent the ship from raising an alarm.

As luck would have it, the ship made it to Block Island at midnight. A whaleboat launched immediately to Newport, Rhode Island, with the news of pirates in the area. Governor Samuel Cranston had the drums beat throughout Newport, calling for volunteers willing to fight. Enough responded to outfit two ships.

Captain John Headlum commanded the first sloop, outfitted with ten guns and manned by eighty volunteers, while Captain John Brown Jr. commanded the second sloop with six guns and sixty men. Both ships were granted a ten-day commission. Heading out the same day as the alarm first sounded, the sloops caught sight of Low's fleet near Block Island. The winds were in the pirates' favor. Unable to catch up to the fleet, both ships returned to Newport without success.

Low and his mates headed to the mouth of Buzzards Bay, Massachusetts, and the island of No Man's Land for fresh water and to catch sheep to bring aboard for fresh meat. Since the militia was actively hunting for him, Low changed his plans and headed to Nova Scotia. On June 15, 1722, he captured the fishing schooner *Mary*, commanded by Captain Flucker and owned by a Marblehead, Massachusetts, merchant named Joseph Dolliber. Low took the *Mary* as his own personal vessel and renamed her *Fancy*; he handed the *Ranger* to Charles Harris to command. Low forced several of the fishermen to join his crew. Among them was Philip Ashton, a 19-year-old from Marblehead.

Receiving the news of Low sailing down toward their vicinity, the city leaders of Boston managed to muster over one hundred men to sail out with Captain Peter Papillion. They did not catch Low, but they were able to save the floundering ship *Rebecca*. Now commanded by Captain Flucker, who previously had commanded the *Mary*, the *Rebecca* was one of the captured sloops Low had permitted to sail home. The *Rebecca* was now crewed by all the fishermen Low had held prisoner from Nova Scotia.

The pirates sailed toward St. John's Harbor, Nova Scotia. They reached the mouth of the harbor on the foggy morning of July 2, 1722, where Low spied a ship he determined was a fishing-trader. Ordering all but six of his men below deck, Low inquired of a small fishing vessel leaving the harbor what ship he had just passed. When the fisherman casually informed Low it was the HMS *Solebay* out pirate hunting, Low wisely turned about and fled. One day later they landed at the small harbor of Carbonear, Newfoundland. After they sacked the entire village, killing many of the townspeople, the pirates torched all the buildings. Heading to the Grand Banks of Newfoundland on July 4, Low's fleet seized and ransacked eight vessels.

At this point Low grew more confident in his ability to capture any vessel he chose. When he encountered two sloops near Canso Island, Nova Scotia, in late July, Low shadowed them. The two ships were on a course heading to Annapolis–Royal Garrison, Maryland. The fact that the vessels were heavy with provisions for the garrison and additional soldiers did not deter Low from his pursuit. For two days and a night he chased the ships, until they managed to escape into the safety of Annapolis Harbor.

Furious that he had lost his prey and knowing that the man-of-war *Solebay* was searching for him, Low decided to make for the Leeward Islands. Miscalculating, Captain Low sailed his fleet into a hurricane. Sailing a wooden ship straight into winds blowing over 100 miles per hour without sinking is a feat unto itself. Sails had to be furled quickly before being ripped to shreds, or they would catch a gust, tipping the entire ship on its side and hurling men into the sea. Masts split in two. Pounding waves rushed across the deck, sweeping men into the churning water. The ship could have been thrown against rock outcroppings, or the hull bottom ripped in two by hidden reefs. Men pumped the bilge continually, ignoring the excruciating pain in their arms and back from the repetition, praying they kept the ship from flooding. Trying to stay as light on the water as possible, the crew threw anything and everything into the sea, including the heavy guns.

After surviving the hurricane, Low's fleet required major repairs and refitting on one of the many secluded islands in the area. Once the vessels were seaworthy, Low took stock of what little provisions remained aboard. His crew continued to attack any and all ships that came within sight, not only for monetary treasure, but also for the necessary supplies to keep the ship stocked.

When in need of fresh water or provisions, one tactic Low successfully employed was the use of hostages. After capturing a vessel, Low would release one crewman to send a message to the nearby town's governing official, demanding that his wish list be granted. If his demands were not fulfilled, Low threatened that his hostages aboard the ship, along with the townspeople, would suffer the consequences. Since the name of Ned Low now struck terror in the minds of everyone, even those who had merely read accounts of the survivors, no one dared refuse him.

Along with fresh water and food, one of the most important items the pirates required was a fully stocked medicine chest. Syphilis was rampant among pirates. In those days mercury, also known as quicksilver, was the only known cure for the disease. With a surgeon who could administer the cure aboard ship, it would temporarily relieve the symptoms of affected individuals. Mercury is now known to be

Captain Edward Low in a hurricane.
CREDIT: UNKNOWN, C. 1734

a highly toxic element; one of the side effects is insanity. Ironically, insanity is also now known as a side effect of syphilis.

A demand for a complete medicine chest was not as uncommon as one might believe. Blackbeard's famous two-week blockade of Charleston Harbor in South Carolina in 1718, and the real threat of killing hostages, was instigated by his demand of a fully stocked medicine chest and not a monetary ransom.

Though there is no proof to the theory, perhaps the violent tendencies Low had displayed since childhood became more barbaric actions in his adulthood because he suffered from syphilis or its cure.

Keenly aware he was being hunted along the Atlantic and West Indies, Low turned his intentions to the Azores. A group of nine islands situated eight hundred miles off of Portugal, that location was a prime target for outgoing ships from Western Europe. On course to the Azores, in the latter part of July, Low captured a French sloop with thirty-four guns and forced her entire crew to sign articles.

Pirates were able to force entire crews to sign pirate articles through sheer terror and intimidation. Once the men signed, they were under the same rules as everyone else aboard. Pirates believed that if a man signed the articles, he had a greater incentive to work alongside, not against, the other men aboard. The fact remained that if the pirate ship was caught by the authorities, the forced men had as much of a chance at being found guilty and hanged as did the more enthusiastic pirates among them. Pirates would separate a captured crew among the various vessels of the fleet. This enabled the pirates to keep an armed watch over the forced men.

Low reached St. Michael Island on August 3, 1722. The fleet, along with the French sloop, entered the island's harbor, St. Michael's Road, to the sight of ten anchored vessels. Not believing his great fortune, Captain Low immediately threatened to kill all aboard the anchored ships if they did not surrender immediately. Seven ships were taken. Of those, four were the *Nostra Dame (Our Lady)*, *Mère de Dieu (Mother of God)*, *Dove*, and *Rose*.

The *Rose*, a Portuguese merchantman loaded with wheat, caught Low's attention. The ship being more to his liking, he had his men dump most of the wheat into the water and transfer the thirty-four guns and provisions from the captured French sloop.

Intent on now burning the French sloop for amusement, Low decided he would release all her crew onto a large Portuguese launch they had stolen—all except the French cook, whom Ned Low declared "was a greasy fellow and would fry well in a fire." That said, Low ordered the man tied to the mainmast and watched gleefully as he was burnt alive on the blazing French sloop. Now in command of the *Rose*, Low handed the *Ranger* to Harris and the *Fancy* to Spriggs.

The brutality of Ned Low and his men against their captives grew ever bolder and more sadistic. Lying in wait on August 20, between the islands of St. Michael and St. Mary in the Azores, Captain Harris in the *Ranger* seized the ship *Wright*. Captain Carter of the *Wright* made the fatal error of attempting to resist their capture. For this act of defiance the majority of Portuguese passengers and crew aboard were slashed and hacked with cutlasses. Low, eager to see what tortures the pirates were inflicting on the prisoners, boarded the *Wright* to observe. As one passenger watched, horrified at the torture of the priests aboard, a pirate drew his cutlass and slashed the man's stomach open, cut out his bowels, and let him die slowly. The pirate simply stated that "he didn't like the looks" of the Portuguese man.

When one pirate swung his cutlass at a passenger, he missed his intended victim and accidently slashed Low under the jaw. The open gash was so severe that Low's teeth and lower jawbone were exposed. Low called for the surgeon to stitch him up. John Hincher, age 22, had graduated from Edinburgh University, Scotland. He had been forced aboard the pirate fleet by Low some time before and was billeted on the *Ranger*. Dr. Hincher spent a lot of his time among the pirates extremely depressed and drunk.

Hincher was in that condition when he boarded the *Wright* to perform the surgery. When Low told Dr. Hincher he didn't like the job he had done with the stitching, Hincher, having been terrified for his life the entire time, finally lost his fear. He balled up one fist and, putting all his strength behind it, struck Low right across his wounded jaw, ripping out all the stitches. Dr. Hincher calmly told Low to "sew up his Chops himself, and be damned." Low's face never properly healed.

When the bloodlust satiated, the pirates voted to cut all the ship's cables, lines, and sails and, with the remaining passengers aboard, set the vessel afloat.

Never remaining in one area too long, they headed to the Cape Verde Islands. Approaching St. Nicholas Island on the morning of October 10, 1722, they came upon the sloop *Margaret*, from Barbados bound for London. Captain George Roberts had made the fatal decision to trade along the islands before turning straight for England. Realizing the ships sailing toward him were pirate, Captain Roberts gave no resistance.

In a stunning reversal of temperament, Low displayed the height of civility toward Captain Roberts. While the pirates looted his ship for days, Low had the captain comfortably billeted on the *Rose*. Low wined and dined Roberts, engaging him in lively discussions of trade, church, state, and family. It is believed that Low treated Roberts kindly because he discovered that Roberts was a married man with a number of children. One steadfast rule every pirate knew aboard any of Ned Low's ships was that no one forced a married man to join. He had to choose the life himself.

Ironically, it was Low's fleet quartermaster, John Russel, who for some unknown reason desired the demise of George Roberts. At any opportunity Russel would verbally attack Roberts, hoping to get the man to reveal anything that could turn Ned Low against him. Days later, after the *Margaret* was stripped of everything, including all her sails, it came time to decide the fate of the *Margaret* and her crew. Low pressed for the life of George Roberts and the return of his ship. Russel acquiesced only when the pirate fleet voted to force all the crew of the *Margaret*, with the exception of two young boys, to sign the pirate articles.

Russel agreed to allow the two boys to board the *Margaret* and help Captain Roberts handle the ship. Russel demanded that not one flask of water or biscuit be placed aboard the *Margaret* before they released her. He would not even allow an old sail to be placed aboard the vessel (Low's suggestion), arguing that the fleet needed all the sails, no matter their condition. Captain Low expressed to Roberts a heartfelt regret at his decided fate, but explained that he could not go against the ship's article of majority vote.

Roberts and his two young servants boarded the *Margaret* on October 29. Russel handed Roberts an old musket and one powder cartridge, as they did for those they would maroon, and set the *Margaret* afloat. The ship managed to eventually run aground on one of the inhabited Cape Verde islands. The older boy, along with the *Margaret*'s longboat, was lost at sea. The younger boy survived. At near starvation and racked with fever, Roberts almost died. They finally arrived in England in June 1725, having originally left London in September 1721. Roberts penned his experiences in 1726 under the title *The Four Years Voyage of Captain George Roberts*. Within its pages he gave a lengthy, detailed account of his time among Ned Low's fleet. Nothing was mentioned concerning the fate of his young servant.

After freeing the *Margaret*, the fleet sailed toward Brazil with the intention of capturing Portuguese merchantmen. They seized a rich Portuguese ship, the *Signiora de Victoria* (*Victory Sign*). After transferring the rich cargo to their ships, the pirates, knowing there had to be money aboard, began to torture the crew for its hiding place. It turned out that once the captain had realized pirates were chasing the ship, he hung a bag with over £1,500 ($750,000) in it out of his cabin window, suspended on a rope. Once the captain knew his ship would be boarded, he cut the rope, dropping the money into the sea. Learning this, Ned Low flew into a furious rage. He had the captain tied to the mainmast and personally severed the man's lips off with his cutlass. Low ordered the lips to be cooked and forced the first mate to eat the scarred flesh in front of the captives. Low then proceeded to kill all thirty-two crewmen and burn the ship.

As the months progressed, Low seemed to develop an acute hatred for all New Englanders who crossed his path. His torturing of those seized became legendary. When he captured the Spanish galleon *Montcova*, Low cut out the heart of the captain and forced a crewmate to eat it before having all fifty-three men aboard slaughtered.

By this time even members of his own pirate crew felt Low's cruelty too much to bear. When stopping for provisions, many who had willingly signed aboard left the fleet. With fewer pirates to manage the sailing, Low continually forced more men into piracy.

Sailing off the coast of South Carolina in June of 1723, he captured the sloop *Amsterdam Merchant*, commanded by Captain John Willard (a.k.a. Wellard) on his return trip to New England. While the fleet was ransacking Willard's ship, Ned Low severed the captain's right ear, split his nose up the middle, and cut him about his body. Low then consented to set the ship adrift.

After the disastrous sea battle with the HMS *Greyhound* on June 10, 1723 (see chapter 11), Low did not consider his desertion of Charles Harris and the pirates on the *Ranger* as a cowardly act. He swore even greater vengeance on any ship for their capture, placing the blame squarely on Captain Peter Solgard.

By the end of July Ned Low seized the ship *Merry Christmas*. He cut ports for thirty-four guns and mounted several swivel guns on her rails. He called himself admiral and hoisted a black flag on her topmast. As a greater number of ships fell under his black flag and more men were tortured, even more of his crew managed to desert. His loyal crew now numbered only thirty.

Toward the end of December 1723, in the dead of night Francis Farrington Spriggs, on his new vessel *Delivery*, deserted Ned Low and set off with his men to sail the West Indies.

In January of 1724 Low captured a ship, the *Squirrel*, commanded by Captain Stephenson. A *Boston News-Letter* article of May 7, 1724, announced the capture of the *Squirrel*, but after that Ned Low's fate is unknown.

There are a number of scenarios of how Ned Low met his fate. Jonathan Barlow, who had been a captive on the *Merry Christmas*, testified that Captain Low had gotten into a fight with his quartermaster and murdered him in his sleep. Upon discovering the murder, his men set Low adrift. He landed on an island and was living with the Mosquito Indians. Others said a French ship had discovered Low adrift in a longboat. Realizing whom they had rescued, they brought Low in irons to the island of Martinique and after a swift trial hanged him. The least likely rumor had him living and sailing around Brazil.

It is estimated that during his twenty-month reign of terror, Captain Ned Low seized over 140 ships.

Captain Willard survived Ned Low's brutal attack. He served as one of the many witnesses against Charles Harris and the pirates of the *Ranger* at their trial.

Philip Ashton managed to escape from Low when the *Fancy* landed in Roatan Harbor, in the Bay of Honduras, while gathering supplies for the ship. With the guise of going into the jungle for fresh coconuts, Ashton managed to stay hidden for five days before the pirate fleet sailed off. Barefoot with only a hat, coat, and trousers, Ashton managed to survive alone on the island without fire or a weapon for nine months before a native canoeing to the island rescued him. He arrived in Salem, Massachusetts, on May 1, 1725. John Barnard published Philip Ashton's memoir, entitled *Ashton's Memorial*, on August 3, 1725. In it he claimed that I "could observe in him [meaning Low] an uneasiness in the sentiments of his Mind, and the workings of his passions towards a young Child he had at Boston (his Wife being Dead, as I learned, some small time before he turned Pirate) which upon every lucid interval from Revelling and Drink he would express a great tenderness for, insomuch that I have seen him sit down and weep plentifully upon the mentioning of it."

On December 7, 1739, Elizabeth Low married James Burt at the Second Church in Boston. Whether she was aware of the fact that her father was the notorious and feared pirate Ned Low is unknown.

Francis Farrington Spriggs exhibited the same characteristics Ned Low admired. He was ambitious, treacherous, and vicious. He was also adamant that the ship's articles that he had signed be precisely followed, and he expected the same of everyone. When one of the pirates aboard ship murdered another in cold blood, Spriggs required the man be executed for breaking the ship's articles. Ned Low, even though he wrote the original articles, would not agree with Spriggs, and the two men engaged in a bitter argument. Not wanting to create a blood battle between pirate crews, Spriggs convinced the men on the *Delight* to follow him. In December 1723, two days after his argument with Low, the *Delight* left the fleet, with the men on board voting Spriggs their captain. They set sail on their hunt for prey.

Soon after, Spriggs captured a Portuguese sloop filled with cargo but little money. For the sport of his men, Spriggs forced the captured men through the "game of sweating."

The pirates formed a circle around the mainmast ringed with lit candles. Stripping their captives of their clothing, the pirates forced each man to run within the circle. As a man ran past the singing and laughing pirates, they would jab and prick their victim's flesh with whatever sharp object they held. One rule of the game was to make sure they did not strike so hard a blow as to kill him. When a captive fell exhausted onto the deck, the pirates would repeat the process with the next person. When the pirates tired of the game, they placed the captives they could not force to join them in a longboat, set the men adrift, and torched the sloop.

On March 22, 1724, Spriggs captured the *Jolly Batchelor*, commanded by one Captain Hawkins sailing from the Bay of Honduras with a cargo of logwood. They looted all the ship's stores and ammunition, throwing all they did not take into the sea along with the logwood. The pirates maliciously smashed cabin windows, cut the ship's cables, and tore down cabin walls. When on March 29 they allowed the ship to continue on its journey, the pirates forced the first mate, Mr. Burrage, and second mate, Mr. Stephens, to remain on the *Delight*.

Another sloop—the *Endeavor*, commanded by Samuel Pike Jr.—had the misfortune to cross paths with Spriggs on March 27. The entire crew was forced into piracy with the exception of the first mate, Dixey Gross. When Gross stated he would not join them, Spriggs announced they would gladly give him "his Discharge, and that it should be immediately writ on his Back." His shirt stripped off his back, Gross was given ten lashes from every man aboard the ship. Among the men forced from the *Endeavor* was a 12-year-old servant named Thomas Morris.

Sighting a sail on April 2, the *Delight* gave chase. After hours matching every maneuver its prey attempted, the *Delight* drew close enough to fire a broadside across the ship's bow. To Spriggs's disgust he had recaptured Captain Hawkins's vessel.

Disappointed they had nothing to loot, fifteen pirates encircled Hawkins and attacked him with their cutlasses. Before a fatal blow was delivered, Mr. Burrage, who had been Captain Hawkins's first mate aboard the *Jolly Batchelor*, begged for the man's life. Spriggs agreed and sent Hawkins down to his captain's cabin for supper. The pirates force-fed Hawkins a full plate of melted candlewax, tossed him around the cabin "to assist in his digestion," then locked him in with their other captives.

Reaching the island of Roatan, Spriggs released Captain Hawkins, an elderly passenger from the *Jolly Batchelor*, Captain Pike and Simon Fulmore of the *Endeavor*, Dixey Gross, and the pirate James

Nelley. Nelley was continually at odds with Spriggs. Captain Spriggs used the opportunity to maroon him with the others. As tradition dictated, the men were given an old musket, a small supply of black powder, and shot. With game plentiful on the island, they were able to survive comfortably. Ten days after they were marooned, a canoe of natives rescued them and brought the men to a more habitable island. The sloop *Merriam*, commanded by Captain Jones, spotted their signal fires, and with the exception of the elderly passenger who died from the ordeal, the remaining men made it to Jamaica and safety.

Ironically, Captain Hawkins and the others were marooned on Roatan Island just four days after Philip Ashton, who had been marooned on the same island for nine months, was rescued and sailing for Boston and home.

Not wishing to careen the *Delight* on Roatan, Captain Spriggs landed on one of the other deserted islands in the Bay of Honduras with plans to sail to St. Christopher Island (St. Kitts). He intended to lie in wait for the sloop *Eagle*. Spriggs had an oath to fulfill. He blamed the *Eagle*'s Captain Moore for the death of his "brother pirate" George Lowther. Spriggs intended to capture the *Eagle* and slowly torture the entire crew to death.

With the island in sight, it was not the *Eagle*, but a French man-of-war that came into view. Spriggs immediately ordered the *Delivery* to tack out to sea, with the man-of-war giving chase. Luckily for Spriggs and the pirates on the *Delivery*, the man-of-war somehow lost her main topmast and was forced to turn back.

Sailing toward Bermuda, Spriggs captured a schooner on April 30, 1724. Once the ship was ransacked and released, her captain, William Richardson, stayed his course to Boston. On arrival Captain Richardson informed the town officials of Spriggs's plan. The *Boston News-Letter* edition of May 21, 1724, reported that Francis Farrington Spriggs planned to "ravage the northern coasts and sink or burn all vessels he took northward of Philadelphia."

Captain Thomas Durell of the HMS *Sea Horse* was ordered to immediately set out to find and capture Spriggs. Captain Durell, as others before him, had no luck in finding Spriggs.

On May 2, 1724, the pirates seized a Boston-owned brigantine, the *Daniel*, commanded by John Hopkins. In the process of pillaging the ship and during a drunken tirade, Captain Spriggs informed Hopkins his plans had changed. He intended to sail the *Delivery* to Newfoundland, where he would increase his crew size. Afterward he'd promptly proceed down the coast of New England in a quest to find Captain Peter Solgard of the HMS *Greyhound* in order to seek revenge for the capture of Charles Harris and his crewmates.

Once again not backing up his threat, Spriggs sailed toward St. Christopher Island, seizing ships. His crews continued torturing their helpless captives regardless of whether the vessels had monetary treasure or hauled cargo the pirates desired.

On June 11, 1724, the *Delivery* seized a boat from Rhode Island on its voyage to St. Christopher Island. In addition to having a hull brimming with fresh provisions, the ship carried a number of horses. With delight the pirates mounted the animals and rode them at a full gallop around the ship's main deck. Amid the cursing, screaming, and laughter the horses panicked, went wild, and bucked the men off their backs. The thrown riders turned on the captured men, whipping and cutting them. The pirates accused the crew of not having boots and spurs aboard, which prevented them from properly sitting on the horses and riding like gentlemen. For all the torture the pirates inflicted on the captured crew, they did not harm the horses.

Spriggs grew ever bolder in his daring attacks. Sailing off Port Royal, Jamaica, he captured a number of fishing vessels. The governor of Jamaica, Edward Trelawny, ordered the two English men-of-war anchored at Port Royal Harbor, the HMS *Diamond* and the HMS *Spence*, to give chase. Believing Spriggs would once again hunt in his old haunts, James Wyndham, captain of the *Diamond*, set his ship's course to the Bay of Honduras.

His hunch proved correct. The *Diamond* arrived mid-September, just as Francis Spriggs and another pirate vessel manned by Richard Shipton were busy attacking ten logwood ships. Taken completely by surprise, the *Delivery* managed to exchange a few gun volleys before Spriggs realized their situation was tenuous. He ordered the ships' men to lower their sweeps into the water and row through the shoals, escaping. (Sweeps are narrow, long canoe-type boats wide enough for one man with one oar per bench.)

Managing to capture a series of ships to sail again as a fleet, Spriggs and Shipton set their course for Cuba. Rounding the western end of the island, they were confronted yet again by Captain Wyndham on the *Diamond*. With the wind against them and unable to maneuver easily away from the *Diamond*, the pirates had no other option but to sail close to the shore on the cape of Florida. Shipton's sloop went aground. Seventy of his men reached land safely but were captured by natives and killed.

During the confusion of the battle and escape attempts, Shipton and a dozen men had lowered a sweep into the water and rowed toward Cuba and safety. Captain Wyndham took Shipton's vessel back to Jamaica as a captured prize. He and his crew received £2,000 ($1 million) in prize money to divide amongst themselves.

Being more skilled at navigation, Captain Spriggs was able to again escape capture, and he somehow managed to rendezvous with Shipton and his remaining men before they reached Cuba. Believing himself invincible, Spriggs returned once again to the Bay of Honduras. Toward the end of December 1725 he continued to capture, loot, and torture any type of vessel that came into his sight.

In April 1725 a ship entered New York Harbor with news that Captain Spriggs, now with a fleet of five ships, was roving the waters, continually searching for prey. Early in May 1725, Captain MacKarty, sailing from Jamaica, reached Boston with news of Spriggs and Shipton. The May 18 edition of the *New England Courant* reported that

Spriggs was amassing a large pirate fleet and intended to attack the entire New England coast.

Spriggs's threatened attack on the New England colonies never materialized. In fact, neither he nor Shipton was ever heard of again. A rumor concerning the men's whereabouts spread through Boston in 1726. Dubious in its accuracy, nonetheless it was published in the *New England Courant* issue of April 30, 1726.

One report stated that the forced seamen on both pirate ships were eventually able to overpower Francis Spriggs and Richard Shipton. They marooned both pirates on an island, where they lived among the Mosquito Indians. The men then sailed the former pirate vessels homeward.

Another version had the HMS *Spence* hunting for Spriggs and Shipton along the Bay of Honduras and eventually chasing them back to the island of Roatan, burning their ships, and forcing the pirates to flee into the wooded interior of the island.

It is unknown how many vessels Francis Farrington Spriggs captured during his pirating days.

CHAPTER THIRTEEN

William Fly

BORN IN ENGLAND, WILLIAM FLY WENT TO SEA AT AN EARLY AGE. He was a man of quick temper and foul mouth. With limited education and limited ability, he did not rise higher than a ship's foremast man or boatswain (petty officer).

Finding himself unemployed on the island of Jamaica in April 1726, Fly met Captain John Green of the sloop *Elizabeth*. Realizing his crew was short men, Captain Green signed Fly on as his boatswain. The vessel's intended destination was Guinea, for a slave-gathering expedition.

It appears William Fly had previously been in the pirating trade, or had considered it for quite some time. Quietly Fly approached a number of the crew and suggested that they take over the *Elizabeth* and turn to piracy. With enough men in agreement, Fly waited for the right moment. On May 27, 1726, while Fly was assigned to midwatch (the four-hour shift beginning at midnight), he—along with Alexander Mitchell, Henry Hill, Samuel Cole, and Thomas Winthrop—approached Morice Cundon, who was on the helm. Placing a pistol to his head, Fly implored Cundon not to make a sound or he would be killed where he stood.

Mitchell and Fly, both with cutlasses in hand, stormed the captain's cabin. They calmly informed John Green they were taking over the ship and then forcefully dragged him on deck. Green begged for his life, pleading that they put him in irons until they could set him free somewhere ashore.

Mitchell grabbed Green and hurled him overboard. In a desperate attempt to live, Green grabbed at the ship's mainsheet (the line that helps control the mainsail). Calmly, Winthrop reached for a ship's boarding axe, cut off Green's right hand, and watched the man plunge into the sea.

The mutineers next brought up the ship's first mate, Thomas Jenkins. Ignoring his pleas, Winthrop cut him about the shoulder and chest with the boarding axe and unceremoniously flung him overboard.

Having chained the ship's surgeon in his cabin during the mutiny, the other men wanted to dispose of him as well. However, Fly argued they might have need of him. The others let him live. Because they had refused to take part in the mutiny, the pirates also bound shipmates Morice Cundon and Thomas Treaton in irons.

Their pirating adventure almost ended before it began. The sloop *Pompey* had accompanied the *Elizabeth* on her journey from England and left Jamaica just a short time after the *Elizabeth*'s departure. The captain, being friends with John Green, sailed by the *Elizabeth* and casually inquired as to his health. Fly, standing on the quarterdeck, replied that Captain Green was well. Believing he did not have enough loyal men aboard to take the *Pompey*, Fly let her sail past.

Changing the captured ship's name to *Fame's Revenge*, the pirates set sail for South Carolina. A mile outside Charleston Harbor, Captain John Fulker, an experienced ship's pilot aboard his sloop, the *John and Hannah*, spotted the *Fame's Revenge*. Setting out in his longboat, Fulker and three of his men, Samuel Walker, William Atkinson, and Richard Ruth, approached the pirate vessel, inquiring if those aboard needed his services.

Fly received them graciously and invited the men down into the captain's cabin to enjoy a bowl of punch. Offering someone to partake in a bowl of punch was considered one of the social niceties of the time. Punch ingredients consisted of hot water, tea, lemon juice, sugar, nutmeg, and strong Arrack rum made from the extracted sap of palm trees in Asia. Once settled and into a few cups of punch, Fly calmly informed Captain Fulker that they were gentlemen of fortune and intended to take over his ship.

Six armed pirates boarded the longboat with Fulker, intending to sail back to the *John and Hannah* and bring her alongside the *Fame's Revenge*. The winds blowing contrary, the men could not get to the sloop and had to turn back.

Not believing Fulker's reason for not fulfilling his orders, Fly had the man stripped and flogged. Fly's ultimatum was simple: Bring him the *John and Hannah* or he would torch the sloop and kill all of them. Once again Fulker took out the longboat. He managed to reach his sloop, but with the winds whipping erratically, his ship ground onto a sandbar and sank. Fly attempted to burn the ship as a gesture of defiance, but the fire went out before the *John and Hannah* became a charred wreck.

Back on the *Fame's Revenge*, Captain Fulker begged that he and his mates be put ashore. Not wanting Fulker to raise an alarm, Fly assured him that once he seized another ship they would be transferred onto her and safety.

The *Fame's Revenge* sailed off. On June 6 they sighted Captain John Gale's vessel, the *John and Betty*. Easily overtaking it, the pirates found only a few old sails and small firearms. Fly forced a number of the crew off the *John and Betty* but decided to let the ship go free.

True to his word, William Fly released John Fulker and Richard Ruth. He also released the surgeon from the *Elizabeth* who had staunchly refused to administer to the pirate. However, Fly refused to let William Atkinson off the pirate ship. He had overheard that Atkinson was a ship's navigator and very familiar with the New England coastline. Fly decided he would be a valuable addition to their crew.

Fly ordered Atkinson to sail the ship to Martha's Vineyard with the intention of putting on water and supplies before sailing to Guinea, but Atkinson deliberately sailed past and into Nantucket Bay. Discovering his deception, Fly grabbed a flintlock and was about to kill Atkinson when Alexander Mitchell intervened. Atkinson was pleading that he had never claimed to know the details of the New England coastline. Mitchell calmed Fly down by reminding him they needed a skilled navigator.

Sensing discord among the pirates, in a brilliant move Atkinson began to ingratiate himself with the other pirates. His plan worked so well that many of them quietly suggested that he become their captain. Atkinson managed to sidestep that conversation and tried to stay out of Fly's way. Fly deliberately kept Atkinson away from the other forced men aboard ship to prevent any surprise retribution.

Fly became increasingly hostile to Atkinson, threatening many times to throw him overboard. Each time his pirate crew prevented Fly from carrying out his threat.

Off Delaware Bay the pirates encountered the passenger ship *Rachel*. Her captain, Samuel Harris, was transporting fifty passengers from Pennsylvania to New York. Finding little of value aboard, the pirates stole what they could from the passengers. After forcing one of the crew, James Benbrook, to join the *Fame's Revenge*, they allowed the *Rachel* to continue to New York.

On June 23 the pirates seized a fishing schooner, the *James*, near Brown's Bank, Plymouth, Massachusetts. In a clever move to save his ship, Captain George Girdler convinced William Fly that his companion ship was in the vicinity and would be a much better vessel for him to take.

Fly ordered Alexander Mitchell and five others of his original pirate crew to board the *James* and pursue the other vessel. This left only Fly and three of his original mates on the *Fame's Revenge* with fifteen unchained forced men.

Atkinson, realizing the ratio was now in his favor, devised a plan. With minimal gestures he alerted two of the other forced men, Benbrook and Walker, to stand ready. His plan was to somehow get Fly off the quarterdeck and away from his flintlocks and cutlass.

Standing at the bow of the ship, Atkinson called out to Fly. He excitedly reported that he had spotted a number of sails on the horizon. He suggested to Fly that they might be vessels containing a great deal of treasure, or perhaps vessels that could easily be taken for Fly to create a pirate fleet of his own.

Fly was reluctant to leave the quarterdeck, stating he could see quite well from his position. Atkinson insisted that Fly could not possibly see these ships from so far away as the quarterdeck. Cautiously, so as to not create any suspicion on Fly's part, Atkinson suggested that Fly approach the bow with his glass (his telescope) and check out the number of vessels for himself.

With a whispered prayer of thanks under his breath, Atkinson watched as Fly walked off the quarterdeck and approached the ship's bow, leaving his weapons behind. In that moment both Benbrook and Walker slowly mounted the quarterdeck, grabbed the weapons, and rushed Fly, overpowering him.

Hearing a struggle above deck, Henry Greenville poked his head out of the forward hatch to check out the commotion. Atkinson struck him unconscious. The other forced men now jumped into action. They rushed below deck and easily overpowered Samuel Cole and George Condick. They clapped all four pirates in irons.

Atkinson took command of the *Fame's Revenge* and, with the other fifteen formerly forced seamen, sailed the pirate ship to Brewster in Barnstable County, Cape Cod.

Their arrival on June 28, 1729 caused quite the stir.

All aboard were transported to Boston and placed in the stone prison to await trial. Immediately, as was their custom, the prominent clergymen of the town descended on the prison to administer to the accused and attempt to save their wretched souls.

The non-juried Special Court of the Admiralty trials began on July 4, 1729. Presiding over the trial were Lieutenant Governor William Dummer and Acting Chief Justice of the Superior Court Samuel Sewall. Also in session were the Boston city councilmen Samuel Adams, David Farnum, Jonathan Loring, and Timothy Proust. The court oversaw four trial sessions.

The first men to appear before the court were the men taken from the *James*: William Atkinson, William Ferguson, and Joseph Marshall. After giving their testimony and having their stories corroborated by their mates from the *James*, the men were acquitted and set free.

The next six men to appear were from the ship *John and Betty*. They were James Blair, John Brown, John Cole, John Daw, Robert Dauling, and Edward Lawrence. Their stories were corroborated by the other men of the *John and Betty*. Being able to prove they did not participate in any acts of piracy but merely handled the ship, the men were acquitted.

The court broke for an afternoon meal, and the remaining accused men were returned to prison, anxiously awaiting the afternoon session. The Reverend Cotton Mather remained with these men.

When court resumed they heard testimonies of support for Edward Apthorp from the *John and Hannah*, James Benbrook from the *Rachel*, and Morice Cundon from the *Elizabeth*. To the prisoners' great relief they were all acquitted and freed that day.

The alleged pirates William Fly, Samuel Cole, George Condick, and Henry Greenville were tried together on the charges of murder and piracy.

Having ascertained that George Condick, age 20, was merely the cook on the *Elizabeth* and consequently on the *Fame's Revenge*, the court acquitted and released him.

Samuel Cole, age 37, pled not guilty. Cole stated that William Fly had forced him into piracy. He swore he never participated in any wrongdoing. Furthermore, he had a wife and seven children and wished, on the mercy of the court, to be allowed to return to them.

Witnesses came forward and contradicted his story. The court did not believe Cole.

Henry Greenville, age 40, also pled not guilty. Greenville stated that he was married and had not participated in murder or piracy. Though not convicted of murder, he was found guilty on the charge of piracy, which was a hanging offense.

William Fly, age 27, to the consternation of all, refused to plead guilty or innocent. He flatly denied any involvement in the deaths of John Green and Thomas Jenkins. He stated defiantly, "I can't charge myself with murder. I did not strike or wound the master or mate. It was Mitchell did it." He refused to acknowledge any crimes, especially avoiding a confession of piracy.

William Fly, Samuel Cole, and Henry Greenville were found guilty. Their execution was set for July 12, 1729.

On July 10, with the exception of William Fly, who refused to attend, the condemned men were brought in irons to the Manifesto Church in Boston and sat through long, grueling hours of sermons on evil, sin, and repentance by Reverend Benjamin Colman.

While Cole and Greenville were truly repentant and feared death, Fly refused to show anything but defiance. On July 12 eyewitnesses reported that Fly, while holding a fragrant nosegay in his hand, cheerfully jumped onto the wooden cart that was to carry the three men to the place of their execution.

As thousands of spectators watched the cart roll by, he glibly called out to those in the crowd who had come to watch his execution. Seemingly uninterested in the last words of his condemned mates, Fly continued to shout comments to the assembled crowd, sniffing the nosegay. When it was time, having climbed to the top of the scaffold, Fly reproached his executioner for having no understanding of his "trade."

Flippantly, Fly examined the rope and, with great flair, playing to the crowd, demonstrated to the executioner how to properly assemble a hangman's noose. After placing the noose around his own neck and tightening it to his own satisfaction, Fly signaled the man to kick the platform out from under his feet.

In all that time, Fly made no statement of regret or remorse and was silent on the matters of hellfire, sin, and repentance. He used an unshakable contempt of his upcoming death as his last defiant act against the social norm.

After the execution and the crowd's dispersal, the three bodies were unceremoniously loaded onto a boat and sailed to Nix's Mate Island in Boston Harbor. There William Fly's body was displayed in a gibbet. As the *Boston News-Letter* of July 7, 1728, reported, "the bodies of the pirates were carried in a Boat to a small Island call'd Nick's-Mate, about 2 Leagues from the Town, where Fly was hung up in Irons, as a Spectacle for the warning of others, especially Seafaring Men; the other Two were buried there."

Reverend Benjamin Colman published his execution sermon under the title "It is a Fearful Thing to Fall into the Hands of the Living God." In the body of the work he stated, "Fly was the greatest Instance of obduracy that has yet been seen among all the Malefactors who have suffer'd in these parts."

The trial of William Fly and his men was the perfect platform for Reverend Cotton Mather to once again preach to the public on the evils of piracy. To Reverend Mather piracy illustrated not only a hatred of traditional authority, by the pirates' creation of their own social government, but a disregard for the God-given hierarchy of traditional social status as well as religious redemption.

For over thirty years Mather attempted to turn a pirate's defiance into public penitence at his moment on the gallows. The reverend made it one of his life's missions to personally visit the condemned. He was known to actually coach the men who would be standing on the scaffold in the way they should act and what their final words or prayers should be.

Mather took great pride in his execution sermons, in which he would in great detail describe the horrific acts the pirates had committed. Realizing he could reach a far larger audience, Mather began to publish not only his execution sermons, but also the conversations he had with condemned men as he accompanied them on their walks toward death.

Cotton Mather believed he was struggling to save men from the fires of hell—and that he could use their wretched examples to illus-

Cotton Mather.
CREDIT: PETER PELHAM, C. 1700

trate God's hatred toward sin and the absolute necessity to be actively sincere in one's repentance.

Reverend Mather had quite the following for his publications. With each edition he believed he was able to reach a greater number of the general public and in so doing turn them from the path of sin. But Fly's defiance to the very end shook Mather. Fly refused to be humbled, even in the last seconds of his life. To Mather's horror he had made a mockery of his mortal soul going to the burning fires of hell.

Fly had also deeply insulted Mather. Fly did the exact opposite of what Mather had advised him to say and do once he walked onto the scaffold. Instead of using his last words to instruct the young people in the audience not to make the same mistakes he had, Fly warned any and all ship captains to treat their crewmen with compassion or suffer the inevitable act of mutiny. In his death speech Fly also refused to forgive the persons who had brought him to what he considered a wronged justice.

Mather published *Vial Poured Out Upon the Sea* after the executions. Mather's self-righteousness could not allow Fly's defiance of God and the laws of society to go unchallenged.

Mather became obsessed with William Fly and his arrogance. Through his writing Reverend Mather was determined to turn Fly from the defiant man the public witnessed on the scaffold into a misguided fool to be pitied. Gathering details from the many survivors of Fly's crimes, Mather began his work by describing in graphic detail the factual acts of piracy that eventually brought Fly to the gallows.

Mather believed by first narrating Fly's brutality so graphically, and then detailing his unorthodox behavior in prison and refusal of religious counseling, he could make the man appear more doltish then daring.

What became of Alexander Mitchell and the other five of William Fly's pirates who had boarded the fishing vessel *James* is unknown.

Appendix A: The Complete Ship's Roster of the Adventure Galley

BELOW IS A LIST OF THE MEN, WITH THE EXCEPTION OF THOSE WHO could write their names only by "making their mark" with an X, who signed the original Ship's Articles of Agreement to sail with Captain William Kidd on the *Adventure Galley*. Taking place on September 10, 1696, the signing was supervised by John Walker, the elected quartermaster. The names are reproduced here in the same order as in the original document.

ON STARBOARD WATCH
(Right side of ship facing the bow)

Robert Bradinham	Herculis Bredsteed	George Bollen
Jan de Roodt	Alexander Milberry	John West
William Beck	John Fling	John Torkeey
Daniel Mokoricke	Georde Sinkler	Henry Sanders
John Weir	Edward Graham	Samuel Bradley
Aldris Saerdenbreek	Peter Hammond	George Tarpole
Archibald B. Bohanan	John Burton	William Skines
Ebenezar Miller	Edward Colliness	James Alger
Edward Roberts	William Percy	Peter P. Rouse
Nicolas Tredgidgen	Elis Strong	Phillip Cunninghame
Yoer Oovrall	James Carr	Thomas Hobson
Robert Hunt	John Pears	John Hunt, junior
Joseph Budden	William Whitley	William Rowls

William Arnett
John Jonson
John Hunt, senior
Cornelius Orvyn
Benjamin Franks
William Wellman
John de Mart
John Parerick, negro
William Hunt

Jan Spons
Isaac Ambros
John Browne
Jacob Conklin
Andries Jeaniszen
Samuel Aires
John Davis
Edward Buckmaster
Covert Baners

Neschen
Hendrick Albert
William Weakum
Nicolis Jennings
Isaac Darnes
Charles Bathurst
Simon de Woolf
John Roberts

ON LARBOARD WATCH
(Left side of ship facing the bow)

John Meade
Bernard Looman
William Moore
James Betles
Joseph Palmer
David Carson
William Bowyer
David Mullings
Edward Spooner
Henry Everate
John Kemble
William Willdey, junior

Harman Buger
Henry Olive
Peter de Roy
John Finely
Casper Spreall
Barnet Higgins
James How
Walter King
John Cullings
Thomas Purdeg
Clexfflders
Robert Ruderford

John Walker, Qtr. Mr.
Hendrickus Cregier
Alex Gordon
Henry Pieterson
John Smith
Noah East
William Turner
Samuel Taylor
Robert Smithers
Joseph Hill
Hugh Washington
Thomas Wright

Richard Basnet
Gabriel Loffe
Peter Lee
Patrick Dinmer
John Fletcher
Robert Clem
Jacob Horran
English Smith
Andrew Calwell

Peter Smith
Morgan Harriss
William Holden
Ery Geyselar
Peter Fewlo
Humphrey Clay
Andrew How
Henry Bainbridge
Jonathan Tredway

Jacol Cornelijs
Alex Mumford
Michael Calloway
William Bowyer, senior
Richard Wildey, senior
Michael Evans
John Watson
Aba Coucher

Appendix B: The Forgotten Ones

Listed below are the names and fates of a number of pirates born, jailed, hanged, or pardoned in the New England area or vanished from the same. These men were not infamous enough for pirate trials to mention them beyond the most cursory of comments or judgments. They are rarely mentioned in history books.

"Aye, But Pirates They Be"

Archer, John Rose: Tried in 1724 in Boston. Hanged on June 2, 1724, at age 27.

Barnes, Henry: From Barbados. Tried in 1723 in Newport, Rhode Island. Found not guilty.

Brandish, Joseph: Born in Cambridge, Massachusetts. Returned to Massachusetts after mutiny on the ship *Adventure*. Arrested. Sent to England along with William Kidd and other pirates on the HMS *Advice*. Hanged in chains at Hope Dock, London, in 1700 at age 28.

Chuly, Daniel: Tried in 1706 in Boston. Fate unknown.

Coward, William: Tried in Boston. Hanged in 1690.

Dole, Francis: Lived in Charlestown, Massachusetts, with his wife when not pirating. Hid James Gillam from authorities until they were tipped off.

Fitzgerald, John: From Limerick, Ireland. Tried in Newport. Hanged in 1723 at age 21.

Fletcher, John: From Edinburgh, Scotland. Tried in Newport at age 17. Found not guilty.

Gillam, James (a.k.a. James Kelly): One of William Kidd's New York seamen. Returned with Kidd in 1699 and changed his name to Kelly. Spent time in the employ of the Grand Mogul. Sent to England with Kidd. While in the Old Bailey awaiting execution, wrote *A Full and True Discovery of all the Robberies, Pyracies, and other Notorious Actions, of that Famous English Pyrate, Capt. James Kelly*. His treatise referenced the unknown Galapagos Islands. Hanged on July 12, 1701.

Goffe, Christopher: A Rhode Island man. One of Captain Wollervy's crewmen. Surrendered in Boston in 1687 and was pardoned. Commissioned by Governor Thomas Hinckley in August 1691 to sail his ship, the *Swan*, between Cape Cod and Cape Ann to intercept pirates.

Halsey, John: Boston born. Privateer turned pirate. Died in Madagascar in 1708.

Harding, Thomas: Tried in Boston. Hanged in 1655.

Hazel, Thomas: From Westminster, England. Tried in Newport. Hanged in 1723 at age 50.

Heath, Peleg: Sailed under William Coward. Tried in Boston. Reprieved.

Henley, Captain: From Boston. Sailed the Pirate Round in the 1680s.

Hore, Captain: Seized ships from New York and Newport. Sailed the Pirate Round in the 1650s.

Jones, William: From London, England. Tried in Newport. Hanged in 1723 at age 28.

Jones, William: Tried in Boston. Hanged in 1704.

Knight, Christopher: Sailed under William Coward. Tried in Boston. Reprieved.

Lacy, Abraham: From Devonshire, England. Tried in Newport. Hanged in 1723 at age 21.

Mundon, Stephen: From London. Tried in Newport. Hanged in 1723 at age 20.

Pattison, James: Tried in Boston in 1704. Fate unknown.

Peterson, John: Tried in Newport in 1688. Pardoned by friends on the jury.

Shutfield, William: From Lancaster, England. Tried in Newport. Hanged in 1723 at age 40.

Smith, John: Tried in Boston. Hanged in 1672.

Sound, Joseph: From Westminster, England. Tried in Newport. Hanged in 1723 at age 28.

Switzer, Joseph: From Boston. Tried in Newport in 1723. Found not guilty.

Thurbar, Richard: From Boston. Tried in Boston in 1704. Fate unknown.

White, William: Tried in Boston. Hanged on June 2, 1724, at age 22.

Wollervy, Captain William (a.k.a. William Woollery): A New Englander. Sailed with Henley off the island of Cigateo (now known as Eleuthera, east of Nassau). Burnt his ship off Newport, where he and his crew dispersed with their booty and vanished.

Bibliography

Anderson, Olive. "British Governments and Rebellion at Sea." *Historical Journal* 3, no. 1 (1960): 56–64.

Atton, Henry, and Henry Hurst Holland. *The King's Customs, An Account of Maritime Revenue & Contraband Traffic in England, Scotland, and Ireland from the Earliest Times to the Year 1800.* Vol. 1. New York: Augustus M. Kelley, 1967.

Beal, Clifford. *Quelch's Gold: Piracy, Greed, and Betrayal in Colonial New England.* Westport, CT: Praeger, 2007.

Bishop, Morris. "On the Grand Account." *New York History* 27, no. 1 (1946): 56–65.

Calendar of State Papers. Vol. 16, *Colonial Series, America and West Indies, 1697–1698,* edited by J. W. Fortescue. London: Mackie and Co., 1905.

Clap, Roger. *Memoirs of Capt. Roger Clap, Relating Some of God's Remarkable Providences to Him, in Bringing Him into New England.* Boston: B. Green, 1731.

Cordingly, David. *Under the Black Flag: The Romance and the Reality of Life Among the Pirates.* New York: Random House, 1996.

Davis, Alice. "The Administration of Benjamin Fletcher in New York." *Quarterly Journal of the New York State Historical Association* 2, no. 4 (1921): 213–50.

Document of the City of Boston for the Year 1886. Vol. 1, issues 1–55 (1887): 232.

Documents Relative to the Colonial History of the State of New-York. Vol. 4., *London Documents IX–XVI, 1693–1706,* edited by E. B. O'Callaghan. Albany: Weed Parsons, 1854.

Dow, George Francis, and John Henry Edmond. *The Pirates of the New England Coast, 1630–1730.* New York: Dover Press, 1996. First published in Salem, MA, in 1923.

Earle, Peter. *The Pirate Wars.* London: Methuen, 2004.

Eckstrom, Fannie Hardy, and Mary Winslow Smith. *Minstrelsy of Maine: Folk-Songs and Ballads of the Woods and the Coast.* Boston: Houghton Mifflin, 1927.

Esquemelin, Alexander. *The Buccaneers of America.* Williamstown, MA: Corner House, 1976. First published in London in 1684.

Gosse, Philip. *The History of Piracy: Famous Adventures & Daring Deeds of Certain Notorious Freebooters of the Spanish Main.* Glorieta, NM: Rio Grande, 1988. First published in 1932.

———. *The Pirates' Who's Who, Giving Particulars of the Lives & Deaths of the Pirates & Buccaneers.* Glorieta, NM: Rio Grande, 1988. First published in 1924.

Jameson, J. Franklin, ed. *Privateering and Piracy in the Colonial Period*. New York: Augustus M. Kelley, 1923.

Johnson, Charles. *A General History of the Robberies and Murders of the Most Notorious Pyrates*. New York: Dover, 1972. First published in London in 1724.

Leamon, James S. "Governor Fletcher's Recall." *William and Mary Quarterly* 20, no. 4 (1963): 527–42.

Marx, Jennifer. *Pirates and Privateers of the Caribbean*. Malabar, FL: Krieger, 1992.

Massachusetts Archives, Volume CVII, pp. 277–79.

Naylor, Rex Maurice. "The Royal Prerogative in New York, 1691–1775." *Quarterly Journal of the New York State Historical Association* 5, no. 3 (1924): 221–55.

Nettels, Curtis. "British Mercantilism and the Economic Development of the Thirteen Colonies." *Journal of Economic History* 12, no. 2 (Spring 1952): 105–14.

Nutting, P. Bradley. "The Madagascar Connection: Parliament and Piracy, 1690–1701." *American Journal of Legal History* 22, no. 3 (1978): 202–15.

Pennypacker, Morton. "Captain Kidd: Hung, Not for Piracy But for Causing the Death of a Rebellious Seaman Hit with a Toy Bucket." *New York History* 25, no. 4 (1944): 482–531.

Publications of the Colonial Society of Massachusetts. Volume 20, 1929.

Rediker, Marcus. *Between the Devil and the Deep Blue Sea: Merchant Seamen, Pirates and the Anglo-American Maritime World, 1700–1750*. Cambridge: Cambridge UP, 1987.

———. "Under the Banner of King Death: The Social World of Anglo-American Pirates, 1716 to 1726." *William and Mary Quarterly* 38, no. 2 (1981) 203–27.

Roberts, Nancy. *Blackbeard and Other Pirates of the Atlantic Coast*. Winston-Salem, NC: John F. Blair, 1993.

Rogoziński, Jan. *Honor Among Thieves: Captain Kidd, Henry Every, and the Pirate Democracy in the Indian Ocean*. Mechanicsburg, PA: Stackpole Books, 2000.

Runcie, John D. *The Problem of Anglo-American Politics in Bellomont's New York. William and Mary Quarterly* 26, no. 2 (1969): 191–217.

Selinger, Gail, with W. Thomas Smith Jr. *The Complete Idiot's Guide to Pirates*. New York: Alpha, 2006.

Snow, Edward Rowe. *Pirates and Buccaneers of the Atlantic Coast*. Boston: Yankee Publishing, 1944.

Stephens, John Richard, ed. *Captured by Pirates*. Cambria, CA: Fern Canyon Press, 1996.

Stern, Philip. "A Politie of Civill & Military Power: Political Thought and the Late Seventeenth Century Foundation of the East India Company-State." *Journal of British Studies* 47, no. 2 (2008): 253–83.

Williams, Daniel E. "Puritans and Pirates: A Confrontation between Cotton Mather and William Fly in 1726." *Early American Literature* 22, no. 3 (1987): 233–51.

Woodard, Colin. *The Republic of Pirates: Being the True and Surprising Story of the Caribbean Pirates and the Man Who Brought Them Down*. New York: Harcourt, 2007.

Index

Primer, Matthew, 108, 110
Prince, Capt. Isaac, 43
Prince, Capt. Lawrence, 123, 124
Prince George of Denmark, 106
privateers, 28–29
    financing for, 106
    See also pirates
Proust, Timothy, 178

Q
Quedah Merchant (ship), 97, 99, 102
Quelch, Capt. John, 103–7, 109–10, 111, 112, 113
Quintor, Hendrick, 122, 130
Quittance, John, 108

R
Rachel (passenger ship), 176
Rackham, Calico Jack, 21
Ragnvald, Rollo, xx
Ramses III, Pharaoh, xvii
Rayner, William, 108
Read, Mary, 21
Read, William, 151
Reeve, Thomas, 149
Republic of the Seven United Netherlands, 33, 34, 37
Rhoades, Capt. John, 35, 37, 40
    and Aernouts, 34–36
    trial of, 38, 39
Rhode Island
    cargo fees of, 55
    pirates in, 29
Rice, Owen, 152
Richardson, Capt. William, 169
Richardson, Nicholas, 108
Richier, Isaac, 56
Roach, Peter, 108, 111, 112
Roberts, Capt. George, 163, 164
Roderigo, Capt. Peter, 35, 36, 37
    battle at Black Point, 40
    trial of, 38, 39
Rogozinski, Jan, xiii
Roman Empire, piracy in, xviii–xix
Rose (frigate), 41
    battle of, 52–53
Rose (ship), 161–62
    See also Low, Capt. Edward "Ned"
Royal African Co., 133, 140
Royal Navy, impressment in, 4–6, 6–7
Russel, Capt. Charles, 133, 134, 135, 138
    and Massey's trial, 140
Russel, John, 163–64

Russell, Edward, 89
Ruth, Richard, 174, 175

S
sailors. *See* seamen
Sands, Edward, 117
San Salvador, xxi
Savage, Abijah, 122, 123
Sawrd, Joseph, 152
Scottow, Capt. Joshua, 40
Scudamore, Christopher, 108, 111, 112
seamen
    conditions on-board ships, 6–7
    impressment of, 4–6
    wages for, xiii–xv
Sewall, Judge Samuel, 51, 109, 111, 112, 178
Sewall, Maj. Stephen, 109, 112
shallop (sailboat), 36
Shapleigh, Major, 36, 37
Shaw, John, 143
Sheean, John, 131
Shipton, Capt. Richard, 171, 172
Shute, Sam, 131
Shutfield, William, 152, 187
Siccadam, John, 42, 51, 52
Sloughter, Col. Henry, 86, 87
Smart, Capt. John, 46
Smart, Capt. Thomas, 131
Smith, Henry, 139
Smith, John, 187
Smith, William, 129
Snelgrave, Capt. William, 18
Solgard, Capt. Peter, 145, 148, 165, 170
    and Low, 149
Somers, Lord, 89
Sound, Joseph, 187
South, Thomas, 131
Southwell, Sir Robert, 65–66
Spain
    control of Spanish Main, 1
    right of sovereignty of, xxii
    treasure ships of, 22–23
    war with England, 2
    See also War of the Spanish Succession
Spanish Main, xxiii, 1, 23
Sparkes, John, 82
Spartaco (pirate), xix
Spriggs, Capt. Francis Farrington, 139, 157, 162, 165, 167–72
    and Harris, 144
    and Nelley, 168–69
Stephens, Mr., 168
Stephenson, Capt., 166

About the Author

Gail Selinger is a maritime historian and pirate expert. She can be seen on the History Channel's *Modern Marvels: Pirate Tech* and *True Caribbean Pirates* and on the American Heroes Channel's program *Fact vs. Fiction*. Her commentary appears on the 20th anniversary edition DVD of *The Princess Bride* and Blu-ray of *Pirates of the Caribbean: The Curse of the Black Pearl*. She is the author of *The Complete Idiot's Guide to Pirates* and lectures on pirates and pirate history. She lives in Redlands, California.